Enjoy Curaçao

Complete and practical travel guide edition 2019/2020

J. van Gurchom
P.C. van Mastrigt
A.A. Steevels

D1563246

Good Time Concepts

Colophon

Published by Good Time Concepts
Amsterdam, The Netherlands

1ˢᵗ edition, 2019
ISBN: 9789492598707
BISAC: TRV007000

Authors
J. van Gurchom
P.C. van Mastrigt
A.A. Steevels

Design
A.A. Steevels

Book layout
P.C. van Mastrigt

Photography
G.A. Johnson

Disclaimer
Although the authors and publisher have taken all reasonable care in preparing this book, we make no warranty about the accuracy or completeness of its content and, to the maximum extent permitted, disclaim all liability arising from its use.

Please send any tips or feedback to curacao@goodtimeconcepts.nl.

© Copyright 2019, Good Time Concepts.

Enjoy
Curaçao

Curaçao is a paradise island with a variety of possibilities for relaxation and enjoyment. Of course, you can always opt for one of the many beaches on the island, but Curaçao has much more to offer. Vacations always fly by before you know it, so this travel guide gives you a practical overview of everything you can do in Curaçao.

About this travel guide

This travel guide was written with a practical approach in mind. In addition to background information about Curaçao, you'll also find a lot of information about everything you can do on the island. From beaches, restaurants and mansions to diving locations, mountain biking and other activities. There are also a number of routes you can take that allow you to discover the most secluded spots on the island by yourself. All in all, this travel guide is compact, easy to carry, and very extensive.

Contents

ABOUT CURAÇAO

CURAÇAO PRESENTS...

ROUTES

PRACTICAL INFORMATION

About
Curaçao

Meet Curaçao

Ask a Curaçaoan what they think of their island and they will give a detailed eulogy about all the beautiful things the island has to offer. The colorful and cheerful shopfronts glistening in the Caribbean sun, reflect the colorful and cheerful nature of the Curaçaoan population. They are rightly proud of their paradise island and it has a relaxed atmosphere. Nobody is too busy and that's just as well. It's hot enough as it is. So sit back, relax and get to know Curaçao.

Meet Curaçao

Multifaceted paradise

Of course, Curaçao revolves around the eternal sunshine, clear blue sea and white beaches. But the island has so much more to offer. Behind the swaying palm trees lies a treasure trove of diverse nature: the rugged and lush Christoffel Park in the west, the rugged seacoast in the north and the secluded areas in the northeast. Not to mention the beautiful coral reefs. The colorful underwater world of Curaçao is in the top five of many lists of favorite destinations.

Location

Curaçao is around a three hour flight from Miami and about 40 miles north of Venezuela, in the middle of the Caribbean Sea. The neighboring islands of Aruba and Bonaire are 50 and 30 miles away from Curaçao, respectively.

The ABC islands are vastly different from one another. Bonaire is pristine and quiet, Aruba is mostly 'Americanized'. Curaçao is the most authentic and largest island of the three, with its 40-mile length and average width of 6 miles. This amounts to an area of about 171 square miles.

Population

Curaçao has around 150,000 inhabitants. Most residents live in the capital Willemstad. There aren't any other larger 'cities' to speak of. There are some small villages and neighborhoods scattered around the island. These are purely residential areas. Unlike in Willemstad, there isn't much to do for tourists there.

Nationalities

It's quite remarkable then, to say the least, that Curaçao still has about 107 nationalities. This stems from the many different colonial countries that have ruled the island through-out the centuries. Most inhabitants are Creole, which is a mix of African and European. The population is the product of a troubled past in which slavery played a significant role. The slavery is still visible and tangible to this day. More on this later in the book. The Dutch, Chinese, Jews, South Americans and Surinamese have also settled here. Whatever their origin, Curaçaoans remain above all Curaçaon: friendly, smiley, relaxed and in love with their island.

Religions

Approximately 80% of the population is Roman Catholic and only 5% of the population state that they do not adhere to a particular religion. Faith, therefore, plays an important role in the life of the Curaçaoans and this is expressed, among other things, in the many churches that can be found all over the island. Yet strangely enough, there is still a short-age of churches, which means that services are regularly held in non-religious buildings.

Tourism

In addition to the local population, Curaçao has around 400,000 tourists annually, more than half of which are from Europe. Around 150,000 tourists come from the Netherlands. There are more than 630,000 day trippers visiting the island with cruise ships. This number is still increasing. Americans are now also visiting Curaçao more and more often, both by cruise ship and by plane. Tourism is therefore one of the most important sources of income on Curaçao and it generates over 850 million dollars annually.*

* Figures refer to 2017, source: Curaçao Tourist Board

Climate

Curaçao has a so-called 'tropical savannah climate': throughout the year the tempera-ture doesn't drop below 82 degrees during the day and (barely) cools down at night to about 77 degrees. Maximum temperatures are between 86 degrees in the spring and 95 degrees in the autumn. The seawater also has a pleasant average temperature of about 82 degrees.

The rain season is in the fall, from October to January. This means short tropical showers and more clouds than during the rest of the year. The humidity rises in August, which can make it feel quite suffocating sometimes. However, the prevailing sun and the cooling wind fully compensate for this, making it a wonderful place to stay during this period. Curaçao is situated favorably in terms of the hurricane zone, the island rarely gets hit by hurricanes. This is also why it falls into the category of the 'Leeward Antilles'.

Because Curaçao is close to the equator, it gets dark early. The sun goes down around seven in the evening and rises around the same time in the morning.

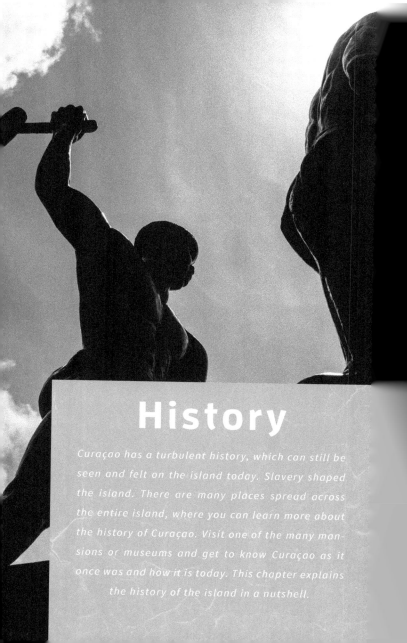

History

Curaçao has a turbulent history, which can still be seen and felt on the island today. Slavery shaped the island. There are many places spread across the entire island, where you can learn more about the history of Curaçao. Visit one of the many mansions or museums and get to know Curaçao as it once was and how it is today. This chapter explains the history of the island in a nutshell.

First residents

Curaçao was already inhabited some 4,500 years before Christ. Columbus, the explorer, described the original inhabitants as "Indians". He was under the assumption that he had arrived in India.

Curaçao was initially inhabited by the Caiquetio Indians, the Arawak Indians later also settled on Curaçao and the surrounding islands. They managed to sustain themselves with fishing and the cultivation of various natural products such as corn. Initially, these Indians lived in caves, until they settled in villages and the caves lost their function as a place to live.

While the original inhabitants of Curaçao were peaceful, around 1400 AD they were joined by some unpleasant guests: the Carib Indians who were notorious for cannibalism and their fighting skills. The Caribbean region is named after this Indian tribe.

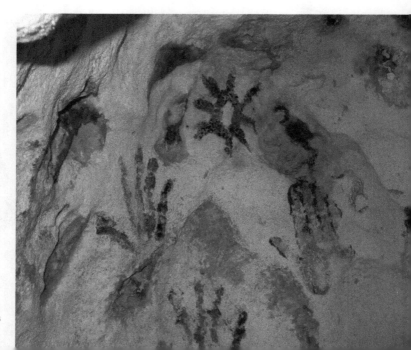

The conquest of Curaçao

European influence

With the arrival of the Spanish conquistadors in 1499, the barbaric practices of the dreaded Carib Indians were quickly brought to an end. Spain invaded the island and although not much was done in the first decades after the conquest, except for some cattle farming (successfully) and agriculture (very little success), in 1525 Curaçao was given its role as one of the most important slave trade centers in this region. This ushered in a dark chapter in the history of the island.

In Europe the eighty-year war broke out and the Netherlands faced a shortage of salt, while salt was badly needed to conserve fish. Salt was available in abundance in the Caribbean and the Netherlands started to play a role in this area.

West India Company (WIC)

In 1621 the West India Company (WIC) was established. Dutch 'hero of the seas' Piet Heyn performed various missions under the flag of the WIC, mostly with success. The icing on the cake was the overpowering of the Spanish silver fleet in 1628, north of Cuba. Eventually fleets of the WIC reached the Venezuelan coast. On the salt pans of Punto Araya, on the other side of Curaçao, they found their new supplier.

In the search for a defensible trade base in the Caribbean, they fell on the strategically located Curaçao which, at that time, was under the rulership of the Spanish. On 28 July 1634, a WIC expedition entered the port of Willemstad. Shortly thereafter, the Spanish surrendered and voluntarily retreated from the island, together with the original inhabitants (about 400 Arawak Indians). The capitulation of Curaçao was complete.

Defense: Fort Amsterdam

After the conquest, work began on the construction of a defensive fort. Fort Amsterdam was built on the tip of St. Anna Bay, in the Punda district. Around it a city wall was erected. The fort and the city wall formed a solid defense of the island. Today the city wall is largely demolished, but the ochre-yellow Fort Amsterdam is still in use. Now there is the Curaçao government and it serves as a governor's residence. There is also a Protestant church.

The fort, the governor's residence and the church are open to the public.

To defend other points of the island against intruders, further military strongholds were built later. For example, Fort Nassau (then: Fort Republic) on the edge of the port of Willemstad and Fort Beekenburg, at the Spanish Waters. These forts can still be visited today and show clear traces from the period of the conquest.

African slave trade

In the first years after taking over Curaçao, the priority for the Dutch was to defend the island against the Spanish conquerors. When the eighty-year war came to an end, and the threat of the Spanish began to decline, the priority in Curaçao shifted from defense to slave trade.

Millions of African inhabitants were captured and brutally deported to the Caribbean. For example, they were shipped to Curaçao where they were traded: almost all slaves that were brought in were also resold. Only a handful stayed behind in Curaçao to work on the plantations.

Not only the trade in slaves was of great economic importance to the Dutch, but more and more trade in all sorts of other goods also increased. This is how Curaçao grew into an important trade center. The port of Curaçao is still the largest seaport in the Caribbean. In 1814 the slave trade was officially abolished, but slavery continued until 1863.

Origins of Willemstad

Oldest neighborhood: Punda

Willemstad consists of the Punda district (derived from Punta, which means 'point') and Otrobanda district (literally translated: 'other side'). The two districts are located on both sides of St. Anna Bay. Punda is the oldest district and was built after the completion of Fort Amsterdam. The district forms the center of Willemstad.

The houses feature characteristics of both the Dutch and Portuguese architectural style, but they are all painted in the typical Curaçao pastels. With this unique mix of styles in combination with the density of the city, Willemstad was included in the UNESCO World Heritage List in 1997.

Working class neighborhood: Otrobanda

In 1707 Punda became quite full, so Otrobanda was built on the other side of St. Anna Bay. Both Otrobanda and Punda consisted of warehouses and houses. After slavery was abolished in 1863 many Curaçaoans settled in Otrobanda as local artisans or small traders.

Chic suburb: Pietermaai

The lack of space in Punda caused the migration of wealthy, mainly Jewish, traders on the island to the Pietermaai suburb at the end of the 17th century. This district is named after ship captain, Pieter de Meij, who built three houses here. To the east of Willemstad there was a small piece of land between the sea and the Waaigat (a branch of the St.

Anna Bay, see the map on page 32/33). Part of the Waaigat was drained, creating a broad foundation for the chic suburb. The rich merchants built their stately mansions here.

Villa district: Scharloo

From around 1870 onwards, a second chic suburb, called Scharloo, was built to the north of the Waaigat. A large part of the Pietermaai residents settled here after the 'orkan grandi' destroyed their homes in 1877. The villas in Scharloo were even more impressive than those in Pietermaai. The business elite spared no costs or effort and built its villas in the Renaissance style, complete with pillars, molded capitals and Spanish patios. On the cool, plant-filled patios, the rich life in Curaçao continued far into the 20th century.

Decline Pietermaai and Scharloo

Mid-20th century, residents migrated to more modern areas on the island. The wages rose and the maintenance of the villas became too expensive for the wealthy descendants. The wealthy families left their homes empty. Pietermaai and Scharloo fell into disrepair. Homeless people, addicts and prostitutes soon found shelter here. In the 1980s Pietermaai and Scharloo were refurbished house by house thanks to the active monument policy and private initiatives.

For more information about contemporary Willemstad, see page 30 and further.

Diversity

As many people visited the island throughout the last centuries and didn't leave, a very diverse population took shape. This is most apparent in the native language: Papiamento. This language originates from several African dialects, mixed with many words from Portuguese, Spanish, English and Dutch. The language was considered extremely important among the slaves at the time of the slave trade: this was the only thing that could not be taken away from them and it enabled them to communicate with each other without the slave owners being able to understand it.

The current population is a melting pot of about 107 nationalities. In the thirties, forties and fifties of the 20th century the island enjoyed huge prosperity. The oil industry created so many jobs that many workers were attracted from surrounding areas. As a result of automation in the oil industry jobs disappeared as quickly as they came, in the second half of the 20th century, and Curaçao struggled with rapidly increasing unemployment.

When in 1985 the Shell refinery threatened to close its doors because of reduced oil production, the refinery came into the hands of Venezuela and the name was changed to 'Isla' (the Spanish word for 'island').

Emergence of tourism

From the sixties onwards, the realization began to sink in that the economic model was extremely vulnerable, which became apparent in the various oil crises. Instead of focusing all the arrows on the oil industry, therefore, refuge was found in the development of various tourist activities. Curaçao has been made more accessible to tourists. In the last decade, many improvements have been made to the infrastructure, the number of hotels and other accommodation has skyrocketed and the airport has been completely renovated.

People are constantly trying to look ahead, but with a few very dark pages in its history and the current difficult economic circumstances, it's easier said than done. The wages on Curaçao are not bad at all in comparison to surrounding nations, but unfortunately there is still a lot of unemployment.

Tourism provides a lot of employment on Curaçao and is therefore an important source of income. The number of visitors to the island has been rising for many years now. In 2017, Curaçao was visited by about 400,000 tourists. In addition, more than 630,000 cruise ship passengers visited Curaçao for a day.

Kingdom of the Netherlands

Over the past decade, much has been said about the role the Netherlands plays in the Caribbean. Many say that Curaçao should become independent, while others claim that they can't survive without the support of the Netherlands.

The Netherlands Antilles were abolished on October 10th 2010. Bonaire, Saba, and St. Eustatius were renamed municipalities of the Netherlands. Curaçao and Sint Maarten have become independent countries within the Kingdom of the Netherlands, following Aruba. This means that Curaçao is no longer part of the Netherlands and is in charge, for example, of education, health care and tourism. The Netherlands remains primarily responsible for defense and Curaçao foreign policy.

Culture

Although Curaçao is officially part of the Kingdom of the Netherlands, it shares very few similarities with the Netherlands: the main difference is probably the lifestyle of the local population, often characterized as relaxed and friendly. The many different nationalities form the population of Curaçao and together they have developed a unique culture over the course of centuries.

Typical Curaçao

Outdoor living

The climate on Curaçao is so pleasant, it's not surprising, therefore, that people mainly live outside. There are always people out on the streets and that makes the island a wonderfully lively place to be. Particularly during the weekends, Antillean families flock to spend their free time together in the open air.

One of the places on the island to meet each other at the weekend is Caracas Bay. It is a meeting place for many families. Until late in the evening they make music and enjoy food from the grill.

Certain beaches on the west side of the island are also popular with locals at weekends, including Playa Abao (Knip). If you like crowds and are curious about the way Curaçaoans celebrate their weekend, then this beach is the place to go.

Music and dance

Music and dance are indispensable for many Curaçaoans. Beloved music and dance styles range from salsa and merengue to jazz and tumba. Tumba is one of the most important dances on the island. Although the name comes from a 17th-century Spanish dance, the tumba originally came from Africa and, under the influence of the merengue, Afro-Caribbean rhythms and jazz music, it has grown into one of the most compelling of all island dances. Today's tumba is best known for its leading role during carnival.

Beyond the carnival, salsa and merengue dominate the island dances. This uplifting, originally Latin-American music movement, has found many musical interpreters on the island of Curaçao. This also applies to jazz music, which is played a lot at restaurants and beach clubs.

Once on Curaçao, make sure to check the readily available PasaBon (events paper) which includes all the events taking place that week.

Food

The many nationalities and cultures here make Curaçaon cuisine extremely diverse. In most restaurants, the cuisine is international and includes most types of food, but the typical Antillean cuisine is characterized by several unique dishes, which often include fish, stewed meat and rice. This is known as 'kuminda krioyo' in Papiamento.

A great place where you can get acquainted with the authentic cuisine is the famous, covered old market: the Plasa Bieu, in the center of Willemstad (see map on page 32/33). In the beginning of the afternoon, when many locals come to enjoy their lunch, it can get very busy here. Plasa Bieu was completely renovated in 2018.

Carnival time

The carnival on Curaçao dates back to the time of the slave trade. The rich plantation owners organized chic balls during the carnival period, where they often spend the evenings together lavishly dressed and in masks. The slaves on the plantation often celebrated a stripped-down version of this type of festival, with their own rituals and costumes. As the slaves were given more freedom and slavery was finally abolished, the workers took to the streets: the street carnival soon became more popular than the masked balls of the small elite group.

Compared to other carnival celebrations in the world, carnival on Curaçao is characterized by the fusion of all different cultures. Each culture shaped the current carnival on Curaçao with its own rituals. During the carnival period that takes place annually from January to the beginning of March, all kinds of parades, parties, competitions and other events are organized. Everywhere you look you can eat, drink and enjoy the music and the joy being had everywhere. The entire island is under the spell of this event of the people.

PARADES

The carnival period ends with two large parades, the 'Gran Marcha' ('big parade') and the 'Farewell Parade'. The Gran Marcha is held on the Sunday before Ash Wednesday, the Farewell Parade takes place on the Tuesday before Ash Wednesday. In the coming years this will be:

	2019	2020	2021
Gran Marcha	March 3rd	February 23rd	February 14th
Farewell Parade	March 5th	February 25th	February 16th

Seú parade

Every year on Easter Monday the 'Seú parade' takes place, also called the 'Harvest Festival Parade' or the 'Harvest Festival'. Until the beginning of the 20th century this procession passed over the agricultural fields. Unique to this parade is the 'Wapa' dance, which imitates movements of sowing and harvesting. Due to the arrival of the oil refinery and the decrease of agriculture, the procession now passes through the center of Willemstad.

Curaçao
presents...

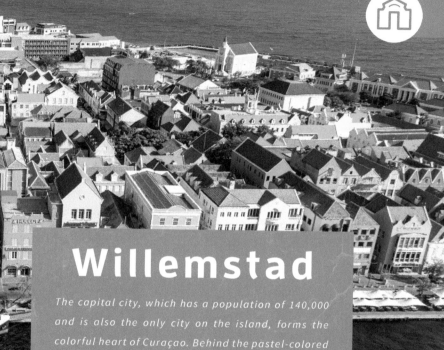

Willemstad

The capital city, which has a population of 140,000 and is also the only city on the island, forms the colorful heart of Curaçao. Behind the pastel-colored façades on St. Anna Bay lies a similarly colorful culture. A carefree local plays their guitar on a bench in the shade, a tourist strolls through the narrow shopping streets and a Curaçaon stirs large pans in the Plasa Bieu. Willemstad is a small city full of contrast. Take the time for a walk through the city and experience for yourself how these contrasts live together under the Caribbean sun.

Willemstad

PRES. R. BETANCOURT BLV.

RING

EEN
ANA
GE

BARGESTRAAT

BOLDINGSTRAAT

SCHARLOOWEG

WERFSTRAAT

VAN DE
ANDHOFSTRAAT

Scharloo

GOSIRAWEG

SCHARLOOWEG

BOULEVARD ABRAHAM MENDEZ CHUMACEIRO

SCHARLOOWEG

PRILESKADE

SYNAGOGE M.I.E.

MARSHE NOBO

P PLASA MUNDO MERCED

RSTRAAT

COLUMBUSSTRAAT

DE RUYTERKADE

PLASA BIEU

waaigat

CONCORDIASTRAAT

PRINSEN STRAAT

WOLKSTRAAT

DE RUYTERKADE

A. DE VEERSTRAAT

WILHELMINA
PLEIN

P

VAN SPEYKSTR.

THEATERSTRAAT

NIEUWESTRAAT

JOHAN VAN WALBEECKPLEIN

ANSINGHSTRAAT

JUL

HENDRIK
PLEIN

P

PIETERMAAI

PIETERMAAI

KAYA WILSON GODETT

PENSTRAAT

Pietermaai

Willemstad is a busy mix of cultures. Locals, tourists and students live side by side here. Where once rich merchants traded, you now have a choice of stores, restaurants and hotels. The port is dominated by huge cruise ships. Terraces sprawl out in the shadow of old warehouses. Locals sell their Curaçaon souvenirs from stalls on the side of the road. In short, Willemstad is a bustling, (mainly) tourist-oriented city. This chapter provides you with an overview of the highlights in each district.

tip! *Everywhere in Willemstad is paid parking. Therefore, park in the large free and secured parking lot at the Waaigat (see map on previous page).*

Punda

Shopping

SHOPPING STREETS - Punda is the shopping heart of the city. In the narrow, car-free streets behind the Handelskade you can find small boutiques, electronics stores, jewelers and perfume stores. Do not expect a spectacular shopping scene here. The stores here are mainly aimed at international tourists who want to buy duty-free cameras, perfumes and jewelry. In particular the striking Penha building on the corner of the Breedestraat is an example of this: traditionally a warehouse and a house, now a department store for duty-free lifestyle products. Furthermore, most stores are located in the Heerenstraat and Madurostraat.

MARSHE NOBO - Marshe Nobo is a round covered market on De Ruyterkade. Here you can shop for vegetables, fruit, fish, Curaçao "sneks" and souvenirs. Much of the same is sold here and as is the case with any other tourist market, haggling is allowed. You can visit the market at the beginning of the afternoon.

Food and drinks

DE BOOGJES - De Boogjes, literally translated as 'the arches', are remnants of the old Waterfort. The Waterfort was built in 1830 as an extra defense fort. The vaulted cellars (popularly known as 'arches') served as storage cellars for ammunition, water and food. Today it houses several restaurants, with terraces overlooking the sea. De Boogjes are located on the Waterfortstraat.

PLASA BIEU - Do as the Curaçaoans do and have lunch in Plasa Bieu, the covered food hall. Plasa Bieu, sometimes also referred to as Marshe Bieu, is highly recommended for those who want to get to know the typical Curaçao cuisine (kuminda krioyo). Upon entering you are instantly met with exotic smells and scents. The hall has several operators, each with their own stall, situated along the length of the hall. Each stall offers its own specialty. When you come here for the first time, don't hesitate to have a look around, before deciding to sit somewhere. It is mainly the Curaçao women who run the kitchen. On the other side of the hall are wooden picnic tables covered with colorful tablecloths in long rows. Found a spot? Then enjoy the special fish dishes such as "bakijou" or "karko" or a "stoba" of goat. Do not forget to add the "pika" from the pots on the table: Curaçao's unique version of a spicy red sauce.

Plasa Bieu is located on De Ruyterkade and is open from Monday to Saturday, from 10.00 am to about 3.00 pm.

Attractions

SYNAGOGUE - Curaçao has the oldest synagogue (1732) in the western hemisphere that has been in continuous use. It seems remarkable, but makes sense when you consider that already since the 17th century, Curaçao has been home to a large Jewish community. The synagogue is beautiful inside. Dark mahogany furniture is in stark contrast to the white walls and copper chandeliers. The whole floor is littered with sand, which symbolizes the Jewish journey through the desert. The Mikvé Israel-Emanuel synagogue can be visited from Monday to Friday from 9.00 am to 4.30 pm. The synagogue is located on the Hanchi Snoa in Punda.

FLOATING MARKET - Around the corner from the Handelskade is the floating market: a series of small boats with Venezuelan market vendors selling their vegetables, fruit and fish. The Venezuelans are far away from home and spend the night in their boats. The boats are hidden behind the stalls, where the merchandise is sold from. When you walk a little further, you get a good view of the boats from the bridge behind the floating market.

BRIDGES - Punda and Otrobanda are connected by the Pontoon Bridge (officially the Queen Emma Bridge). A unique bridge construction that floats on the water by means of floating platforms (pontoons). If a ship has to pass by, the bridge will "sail" open by way of a driving engine at the end of the bridge. Hikers who want to cross don't have to wait, they can use the free ferry services that sail back and forth. Because the pontoons drift on the water, it feels like you are onboard a boat when you cross this bridge.

In order to efficiently manage car traffic from one side to the other, in 1974, the 183-feet high Queen Juliana Bridge was built. Large ships can easily sail through underneath the bridge. The view over Willemstad from this height is breathtaking. Unfortunately, it is not allowed to go on the bridge on foot or stand still with the car.

Otrobanda

Shopping

BREEDESTRAAT - Breedestraat is the main shopping street in Otrobanda. Local residents do their daily shopping here. No international brands or large perfumeries here, but rather typical Curaçao boutiques, hair salons and sneks (snacks), complete with painted store fronts and antique signs.

RIFFORT - In the 19th century, the riffort was built as an extra defense in the other corner of St. Anna Bay, opposite Fort Amsterdam. The fort wall is still (mostly) there. You can climb on top of the wall via a staircase. From the fort wall you have a beautiful view over the St. Anna Bay and the sea. The Renaissance Mall and Rif Fort are located in the Riffort, complete with resort, casino and cinema. There are also several stores, restaurants and terraces here. Here is also the memorial of the slave revolt of 1795.

DE ROUVILLEWEG - A little further along the St. Anna Bay you'll find a row of stalls lined up at De Rouvilleweg. Buy your typical Curaçao souvenirs here or have a personal name-plate painted for the front door at home. Behind the De Rouvilleweg is the Brionplein. Not a particularly special square, but it's home to the statue of the Curaçao independence fighter Pedro Luis Brion.

Food and drinks

SNÈKS (SNACKS) - In Otrobanda, for a "pasteichi", a sandwich "karni stoba" or other Curaçao snacks, you go to a "snèk", a small eatery in the street. Do as the locals do and make a pit stop at a snèk to refuel. Fortunately they're not restricted to Otrobanda, there are various snèks scattered around the island.

Attractions

tip! **KURÀ HULANDA** - Kurà Hulanda means 'Dutch heritage' and is an initiative by the Dutch-man Jacob Gelt Dekker, who wanted to restore and honor a part of the dilapidated Otro-banda. The area of Kurà Hulanda consists of a hotel and a museum. The hotel contains the original houses that were built there in the past. The cottages have been completely restored and now serve as hotel rooms. It gives you a good idea of what it used to look like. In the evening you can regularly enjoy live music on the square amid the houses.

The museum tells you about the history of slavery in Curaçao and the Caribbean. A visit to the museum is an absolute must to learn more about the tough slave trade history of the Netherlands and Curaçao. For detailed information, see the chapter Tourist attractions, page 79.

Pietermaai and Scharloo

Pietermaai and Scharloo are, as previously described, traditionally the more upscale neighborhoods in Willemstad. The prosperous merchants built their imposing mansions here. After the decline of these districts in the 20th century, Pietermaai and Scharloo were gradually rebuilt. Today, the neighborhood improvement is still underway and many houses here have had their old elegance restored.

Nice to do

SHOPPING, EATING, SLEEPING - Pietermaai is where you mainly come to dine, stay in one of the boutique hotels or to view the beautifully restored mansions. In the chapter Restaurants you will find more information about the different restaurants and bars in Pietermaai and Scharloo, starting on page 108.

Sights

HOUSES - Take a walk through these neighborhoods in the afternoon and view the carefully restored colonial façades and murals. Here and there you'll still come across the odd dilapidated building, which gives the whole a raw edge and also shows that it is a neighborhood in development.

Beaches

The beaches of Curaçao are of the finest white sand, clear blue bays, where schools of brightly colored fish pass by the snorkelers. But no beach is like the next. The beaches differ from each other in terms of atmosphere and facilities. This travel guide gives you a complete overview of the range of beaches at all times, divided into three areas: beaches in the west, middle and east of Curaçao. Experience for yourself how relaxing life can be on the many paradise beaches.

PLAYA KALKI

Westpunt

PLAYA GRANDI

PLAYA FORTI

GROTE KNIP

Lagun

KLEINE KNIP

CHRISTOFFEL
PARK

Barber

PLAYA JEREMI

Jan Donker

PLAYA LAGUN

SANTA CRUZ

Soto

Weg naar Santa Cruz

PLAYA SANTA MARTHA

Tera
Korá

Weg naar Westpunt

Sint
Willibrordus

Jan
Kok

Grote Berg

CAS ABAO

PORTOMARI

Jan Kok Baai

Bullenbaai

Weg naar Bullen

DAAIBOOI

KOKOMO BEACH
(VAERSENBAAI)

Overview of beaches on Curaçao

HATO AIRPORT

naar Westpunt

Franklin D Rooseveltweg

Winston Churchillweg

Gosieweg

Brievengat

Schottegatweg

Ring

Santa Catarina

Weg naar Santa Catarina

Sint Jorisbaai

Santa Rosaweg

Santa Rosa

Santu Lораweg

Sint Michiel

Piscaderabaai

WILLEMSTAD

Schottegat

Caracasbaaiweg

Weg naar Fuik

Blauwbaai

Piscadera

Otrobanda

Ring

Salña

Punda

Pietermaai

Lagun Jan Thiel

Jan Thiel

Spanish Water

Oostpunt

Caracasbaai

Santa Barbara

PIRATE BAY

JAN THIELBAAI
ZANZIBAR
PAPAGAYO

BLUE BAY

MARIE PAMPOEN

MAMBO BEACH BOULEVARD
MOOD BEACH,
CABANA BEACH,
WET & WILD BEACH CLUB,
MADERO OCEAN CLUB,
ALOHA BEACHBAR

Good to know

Some beaches are accessible and free of charge, on some of the other beaches you have to pay. Sometimes a beach bed is included in the entrance fee, elsewhere you pay for it separately. Prices range from USD 3 to USD 6 (NAF 5 to NAF 10) per person for access and the same for beach beds. The prices change regularly. We therefore don't mention specific prices per beach, just whether or not you have to pay for it.

Index

We use the following icons to display the information and facilities per beach.

 Paid access   Shower available   Catering available

 Beach chairs available   Toilet available   Happy hour

Beaches in the west

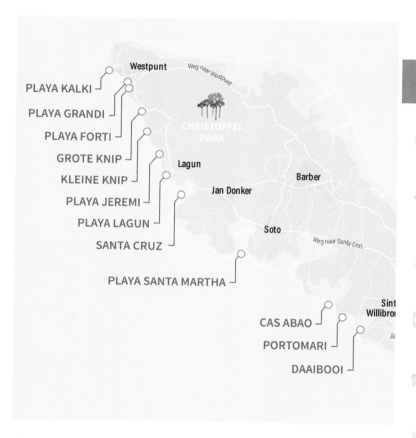

PLAYA KALKI
PLAYA GRANDI
PLAYA FORTI
GROTE KNIP
KLEINE KNIP
PLAYA JEREMI
PLAYA LAGUN
SANTA CRUZ
PLAYA SANTA MARTHA
CAS ABAO
PORTOMARI
DAAIBOOI

Westpunt
Weg naar Westpunt
CHRISTOFFEL PARK
Lagun
Jan Donker
Barber
Soto
Weg naar Santa Cruz
Sint Willibro
Ja

The west (Banda Abao) has the most peaceful and natural beaches. Tucked behind green hills and rocks. Here you'll also find the best snorkeling and diving spots. They are the finest examples of what a tropical beach should look like. Below you will find an overview of all beaches in the west - from Westpunt along the south coast, towards the east.

Playa Kalki

Playa Kalki is the westernmost beach on Curaçao and owes its name to the limestone cliffs that surround the beach. The bay has one of the most beautiful reefs on the island and is therefore very popular with avid snorkelers and divers. With a bit of luck you can spot a sea turtle here. At the top-end of the beach on the cliff is the Kurá Hulanda resort. From the resort you have a beautiful view of the bay and the Caribbean Sea. Also a great place to enjoy a big lunch.

Playa Grandi

Playa Grandi (or Playa Piskado) is a quiet beach. The sand is a bit coarser, dotted with loose stones and some occasional small rock formations. Playa Grandi is mainly a place for snorkeling (turtles almost guaranteed) or to see mooring fishing boats and fishermen who portion large fish on the beach, available for sale. On the beach there are some Machineel trees that provide the necessary shade. There's a small snackbar which is open during the weekends.

Playa Forti

Playa Forti is a small beach with dark sand and loose stones. The beach is quiet, you can eat local cuisine at the restaurant on a 40-feet high cliff. Playa Forti particularly attracts adventurers who dare to jump from this magnificent cliff. Entirely at your own risk, but refreshing and, above all, exciting.

Playa Abao (Grote Knip)

Playa Abao (or Grote Knip) is one of the most popular beaches for both locals and tourists (especially during the weekends). It is situated in a sheltered, green bay, with high cliffs on both sides. The fine sand is bright white and the beach slowly descends into the calm and crystal clear water. It's a nice place to go snorkeling, around the cliffs. For the experienced swimmer there is a beautiful reef a little further into the sea, but watch out for boats and jet skis that sometimes sail into the bay.

Kenepa Chiki (Kleine Knip)

Next to Grote Knip is Kleine Knip (or Playa Kenepa Chiki). Kleine Knip is literally the little brother of Grote Knip. You can go snorkeling along the rocks and there is a beautiful reef further up into the sea. There are a few more stones on the beach and a lot of washed up coral. Water booties can therefore be useful. The beach offers very little in terms of facilities and is often a lot quieter than Grote Knip.

Playa Jeremi

If you really want to escape the crowds and immerse yourself in the nature, Playa Jeremi is the place to go. There are no facilities on this hidden beach and there is only one parasol. The beach is a bit rougher, the water is crystal clear. It is also an ideal diving and snorkeling spot. Even within the bay you can regularly spot turtles. Playa Jeremi is the place to let the unspoiled nature of Curaçao really soak in.

Playa Lagún

Playa Lagún is situated in a deep cove with high rocks on both sides. The sea in the bay is therefore calm. The beach gradually declines and there are a number of stone formations on the bottom. You'll also encounter the occasional fishing boat on the beach and some palapas for shade. This gives the whole image an idyllic appearance. Playa Lagún is relatively quiet, although it has been discovered by more and more people in recent years.

Santa Cruz

The bay in Santa Cruz has a deep, spacious sandy beach with picnic tables and parasols that provide shade. Furthermore, Captain Goodlife is here. This true bon vivant will take you to the most beautiful places on the island by taxi boat, at a low price. Imagine remote beaches, caves and amazing snorkeling and diving spots. At his jetty at the beach he often prepares a fresh meal. For more information and reservations see facebook.com/capt.goodlife/

Playa Santa Martha

Santa Martha is a 'forgotten' bay. Very few are aware of it and it is therefore far from busy. On the beach are the remains of an abandoned resort, which gives it a surreal look. And the view of the bay, on the way there, is more than worthwhile. It's not easy to find: take the exit in Soto to Groot Santa Martha mansion and continue along the bumpy road past the mansion, past a resort until you reach the deserted resort. The washed up coral means it's not ideal, but swimming is fine.

Cas Abao

Cas Abao is in many a top 3 list. The fine sand here is whiter than white and the calm water is clear blue. The bay is elongated and the beach gently slopes into the sea. The many palms provide shade. The underwater world is also particularly beautiful here, even manta rays can sometimes be seen here. Furthermore, there are plenty of facilities: you can have a massage at the hut on the beach or go kayaking in the bay. Note: the access road is in very bad condition. You pay access for each car and sun lounger.

PortoMari

PortoMari is a real evergreen: the bay is long with fine, white sand and the calm sea is crystal clear here. The beach is nicely sheltered behind a row of green bushes and trees that provide plenty of shade. The restaurant has an extensive but simple menu and cozy beach bar. A reef has been laid out in the water in the form of reef balls, which attract an array of fish. PortoMari is beautiful and comfortable and can therefore get very busy. For a good spot in the shade it is best to get there early.

Daaibooi

Daaibooi is one of our personal favorites. The beach is deep and spacious and is sheltered between high rocks. It's a good place to go snorkeling along the rocks. There are some palapas and palms here for shade. Tips: make sure to drink a "coffee Kees" here, the owner's special. Or go barbecuing, which is allowed here. Daaibooi is a real family beach, a lovely place to meet at the weekend. Tip: walk up over the rocks and enjoy the beautiful view over the bay.

Beaches in central Curaçao

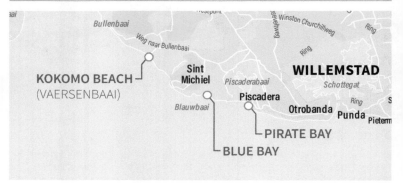

This region is located just west of Willemstad. There are three famous beaches in this area, which are fully equipped in terms of facilities. That makes these beaches especially attractive among tourists. In particular at the weekend, it can be busy.

Kokomo Beach (Vaersenbaai)

In 2011, the owner at Kokomo Beach completely renovated the formerly dilapidated Vaersenbaai and started a beach spot, complete with beach beds, palms and tarps for shade. In the weekends you have live bands and parties. On Sundays it is happy hour from 5pm to 6pm. You can not bring your own food and drink here on the beach, but there's plenty available to order. The coastline is quite rocky, but in the water around the corner is a beautiful reef.

Blue Bay

Blue Bay (or Blauwbaai) is part of the Blue Bay Resort but is accessible to everyone. The spacious beach includes private cultivated palms and large umbrellas for shade. The beach bar has an extensive snack menu which can be served on the beach. You can also dine extensively on the beach (make sure to have appropriate clothing). At the white cottage in the back you can get a massage. Every Friday there is live music during happy hour between 5pm and 7pm. There's a nice playground for children next to the entrance.

Pirate Bay

The beach restaurant at Pirate Bay has a nice intimate atmosphere and has excellent international cuisine. The interior is reminiscent of a film set from Pirates of the Caribbean. The beach itself is quite small. To the right of the beach is a long pier, at the end there's a staircase that leads into the water. Pirate Bay regularly organizes live performances, dance workshops, salsa evenings and a daily happy hour from 5pm to 6pm. This is also a popular wedding location.

Beaches in the east

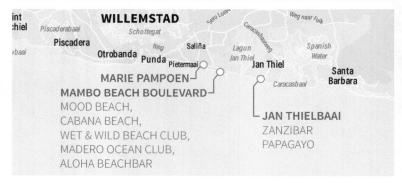

WILLEMSTAD

Piscaderabaai
Schottegat
Piscadera
Otrobanda
Punda
Pietermaai
Ring
Saliña
Lagun
Jan Thiel
Jan Thiel
Santa Barbara
Spanish Water
Caracasbaai

MARIE PAMPOEN
MAMBO BEACH BOULEVARD
MOOD BEACH,
CABANA BEACH,
WET & WILD BEACH CLUB,
MADERO OCEAN CLUB,
ALOHA BEACHBAR

JAN THIELBAAI
ZANZIBAR
PAPAGAYO

This region is located just east of Willemstad. The eastern beaches are the most touristy beaches, laid out and maintained by different beach clubs and resorts, all except for the city beach Marie Pampoen. Although there are no idyllic bays and hidden beaches, there are many facilities that make a day at the beach very comfortable and relaxing.

Marie Pampoen

A city beach about 3/4 mile east of Willemstad. On weekdays it is quiet here and at weekends it gets busy. There is a special reef which consists of old-timer car wrecks, which have been sunk to create an artificial reef. Therefore, two small diving schools are located here. Highly recommended is the Sea Side Terrace, a restaurant which serves local cuisine and fresh and locally caught fish. For more information see page 116.

Mambo Beach Boulevard

Mambo Beach Boulevard is the tourist heart of the island. There's lots to enjoy throughout the day here on (and surrounding) this busy beach. There is a brand new shopping mall complete with stores, restaurants and bars. You can swim in the sea or in the pool on the beach. Furthermore you can do water sports to your heart's content and the beach is fully equipped when it comes to facilities. On the beach you will find several beach clubs side by side. Especially during the weekend, you can take advantage of the many happy hours on offer, see page 124.

Jan Thielbaai

A popular beach with all imaginable facilities with several restaurants and a beach bar with luxurious beach beds. There is a spa to get a massage or pedicure, a beach shop and the Scuba diving school. Beach club Zanzibar is very pleasant during the weekly happy hour on Saturday. The beach is about 5 feet above the sea, like a kind of quay. The beach runs directly into the water. You'll find various vacation resorts and restaurants near this bay.

Things to do

When it's time for action, Curaçao has more than enough to offer. For example, take the 1200-feet-high climb to the top of the Christoffel Mountain or go on jeep safari through the rugged west of Curaçao. Find out more about Curaçao's past and plan a route along the imposing mansions. Prefer the water? Bounce along at a speed of 60 mph across the sea with a powerboat or go windsurfing on the Spanish waters. With this travel guide you have a complete overview of all activities and sights on the island.

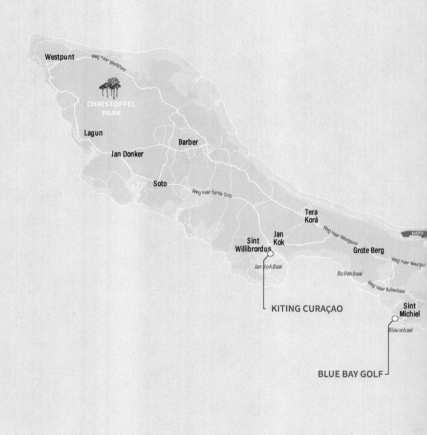

Westpunt

Weg naar Westpunt

CHRISTOFFEL PARK

Lagun

Jan Donker

Barber

Soto

Weg naar Santa Cruz

Tera Korá

Weg naar Westpunt

HATO

Sint Willibrordus

Jan Kok

Jan Kok Baai

Grote Berg

Weg naar Westpu...

Bullenbaai

Weg naar Bullenbaai

KITING CURAÇAO

Sint Michiel

Blauwbaai

BLUE BAY GOLF

Overview of things to do on Curaçao

CURAÇAO GOLF & SQUASH CLUB

DASIA CURAÇAO
MOUNTAINBIKES & RACING BIKES

WANNABIKE CURAÇAO

NIX KITE CURAÇAO
KITESURFING

SAIL ADVENTURE CURAÇAO
MOTOR BOATS, SAIL BOATS & SAILING LESSONS

AIRPORT

Franklin D. Rooseveltweg

Winston Churchillweg

Brievengat

Kaya

Ring

Santa Catarina

Weg naar Santa Catarina

Santa Rosa

Sint Jorisbaai

Piscaderabaai

WILLEMSTAD

Schottegat

Santa Rosaweg

Senú Lora weg

Caracasbaaiweg

Weg naar Fuik

Piscadera

Piscadera

Otrobanda Punda

Ring

Saliña

Pietermaai

Lagun
Jan Thiel

Jan Thiel

Caracasbaai

Spanish
Water

Santa
Barbara

Oostpunt

OLD QUARRY GOLF COURSE

WINDSURFING CURAÇAO
*WINDSURFING, SUPBOARDING, WAKEBOARDING,
HIKING & BIKING*

BLUEFINN CHARTERS
CATAMARAN TRIPS

ZAPATA FLYBOARD CARIBBEAN
*FLYBOARDING, WINDSURFING, SUPBOARDING,
WAKEBOARDING, HIKING & BIKING*

Things to do on land

Below are some suggestions for if you want to alternate between beach days on Curaçao and some more active days.

Hiking

The landscape on Curaçao is ideal for hiking. There are many signposted hiking trails (about 40) that can be found all over the island. A large portion of the walking routes has been mapped out by Stichting Uniek Curaçao. You can discover it on your own or join an organized tour.

Below are some tips from experienced hikers on Curaçao:
- Do not go alone, find one or more people or go out with an experienced hiker. An experienced hiker knows all the corners of the island and can show you the most beautiful places.
- Protect yourself from the sun and the heat with a hat and sunscreen. Wear sturdy shoes, some paths are rocky. Take enough water.
- The ideal time for hiking is in the early morning from 7am or in the afternoon from 4pm.
- Handy to take with you: a cane and a flashlight, for caves and when the hike runs into the evening and it starts to get dark.
- Try to be back before dark.
- Never touch the fruits and leaves of a manzanilla tree. They are extremely toxic.

The landscape on Curaçao is quite accessible. The vegetation is very diverse and consists of much more than sand flats and cacti. A good website with extensive hiking reports is Curacaopictures.com/en.

City walks through Willemstad

 DUSHI WALKS - There are some organized walking tours through Willemstad. You walk through the as yet undiscovered streets in Punda, Otrobanda and Scharloo. The tour explains the origin of the city and the architecture. Dushi Walks leads you past known and unknown city art and special buildings. Nice to know: a large part of the proceeds will be spent on all kinds of basic necessities for the 'cholèrs' ('tsjollers') in the city: the homeless.

Organized walks, hiking trails and reports can be found on:
- Curacaohikinganddiving.com
- Curacaopictures.com

Golf

A popular sport on Curaçao is golf. There are several golf courses on the island:

BLUE BAY BEACH & GOLF RESORT - You can play the 18 holes on this course without a membership. It's also possible to improve your skills at any level, through a training course in the sport of golf or a separate lesson. This golf course is challenging for every level and has a beautiful location with a view of the sea.

 Blue Bay Beach & Golf Resort
Website: golf.bluebay-curacao.com | Tel.: +599 9 868 1755

OLD QUARRY GOLF COURSE - According to the golf connoisseurs it's a gem among golf courses. The course was designed by the well-known golf course architect Pete Dye and is part of the chic Santa Barbara Beach & Golf Resort in the east of Curaçao. The course consists of 18 holes and gives a nice view over the Caribbean Sea and the Spanish Water.

Ⓘ **Old Quarry Golf Course**
Website: oldquarrygolfcuracao.com | Tel.: +599 9 840 6886

CURAÇAO GOLF & SQUASH CLUB - Also an 18-hole golf course, located next to the oil refinery in Willemstad. Not the most beautiful location of the three, but central and surrounded by greenery, exotic birds and iguanas.

Ⓘ **Curaçao Golf & Squash Club**
Website: curacaogolf.com | Tel.: +599 9 737 3590

Mountain biking

Mountain biking is very popular on the island. There are at least 180 miles of signposted cycling routes that have been set out for both beginners and advanced cyclists. You can discover these routes independently or with a guide. For those who don't want to miss anything, a guided tour is recommended. You'll come across places that are inaccessible by car, including the rugged coastline or the sandy roads that run over the old plantations. Or you can take a route along the ancient forts, through mangrove forests and along secluded beaches. Along the way there are many exotic birds and other animals to spot. Below are some addresses where you can book tours and rent bikes.

Keep the following tips for a carefree trip: you're obliged to wear a helmet while cycling on Curaçao. It is highly recommended to go early in the morning or in the afternoon, when the temperatures are the most pleasant. When you are out all day long you can, for example, cycle to a beach in the morning, spend the afternoon there and go back in the afternoon. Make sure you are back before dark, take enough food and drink with you and don't forget your sunscreen.

🚲 **For a guided tour, go to WannaBike Curaçao**
Address: Caracasbaaiweg 340, Hofi Granville | Website: wannabike.com | Tel.: +599 9 527 3720

🚲 **The biggest rental store for mountain bikes and racing bikes is Dasia Curaçao**
Address: Specialized Concept Store, Kaya Flamboyan 1a, Curaçao | Website: dasiacuracao.com | Email: info@dasiacuracao.com | Tel: +599 9 737 1112 | Mob: +599 9 525 1112

Things to do in/on the water

A tropical island is of course the perfect place to practice all kinds of water sports. Every imaginable water sport is represented here.

Windsurfing

Curaçao has good spots for windsurfing, including the Spanish Water and Sint Jorisbaai. Windsurfing Curaçao is located at the Spanish Water. You can rent equipment and take lessons, where fast results are guaranteed: you'll be able to stand on your board within the hour. The Spanish Water involves relatively calm inland water where there are virtually no waves. It is on the southeast coast of the island. Sint Jorisbaai is also an inland waterway and is on the northeast coast of the island. Here the winds are a bit stronger than at the Spanish Water.

🏄 **Windsurfing Curaçao**
Open: daily 10AM to 6PM | Address: Caracasbaaiweg (turn left at the end of the road)
Website: windsurfingcuracao.com | Tel.: +599 9 738 0883

Surfing

Wave surfing isn't that big on Curaçao. There are two spots where you can venture to the waves. Playa Kanoa on the rugged north coast is a good surf spot. The ever-present trade winds ensure good waves. A disadvantage is that Playa Kanoa has a reef break instead of a beach break. The coastline isn't a sandy beach, but a reef. Coral is sharp and it's easy to injure yourself. Some experience and alertness are therefore required. Playa Kanoa is an ideal surf spot for the experienced and adventurous surfer. Equipment can be rented on the beach and you can take lessons.

There are also surf spots on the coast of Klein Curaçao. But the weather and water conditions are not always ideal here.

Kite Surfing

Curaçao is not the most popular spot for kitesurfers, but it is gradually gaining ground. Especially for beginners, Sint Jorisbaai and inland waters at Sint Willibrordus are ideal kitesurfing spots. The water here is quiet and there is always a strong wind, especially in the months between February and August. Klein Curaçao is a nice spot for experienced kite surfers. The waves are much higher here and there are side winds. In addition, you can also go kitesurfing at the Marriott resort located next to the Piscadera Bay and at the beach of Marie Pampoen.

ⓘ **For lessons in Sint Joris Bay: nixkitecuracao.com**
Instructor Nick Brouwer: Tel.: +599 9 520 2562 / +599 9 738 5544 | Email: nixkitecuracao@gmail.com.·

ⓘ **For lessons in the bay at Sint Willibrordus: kitingcuracao.com**
Tel.: +599 9 661 3109 | Email: info@kitingcuracao.com.

Flyboarding

An increasingly popular sport is flyboarding. Flyboarding is best described as 'hovering' above water with a board with hoses connected to it. These hoses allow you to build up water pressure by 'accelerating'. The power of the water makes you float above the water. The water power is driven by a kind of jetski (a 'waverunner'). If you hover above the water, it is important to keep your balance, so that you keep 'flying'. But according to Zapata you can get the hang of it in no time. Flyboarding can be done at Zapata (age 14+), and it has a capacity of a maximum of 220 lbs (100 kg).

ⓘ **Zapata Flyboard Caribbean**
Open: daily 10AM to 6PM | Address: Jan Thielbaai, next to Zanzibar
Facebook.com/zapataflyboardcaribbean | Tel.: +599 9 512 3359 | Email: flyboardcuracao@gmail.com

Powerboat

Experience 600HP on the Caribbean Sea. It's now possible to book a boat trip on a rib powerboat and view the coast of Curaçao with a healthy dose of adrenalin. You get to view beautiful places while maneuvering between the waves. A roller coaster pales in comparison. If you're lucky, the dolphins will join you alongside the boat as you race across the sea.

(ⓢ) **Powerboat Caribbean**
   Look for different tours and locations on www.powerboat-caribbean.com or call +599 9 566 9697

Supboarding

Another fast-growing water sport is supboarding, or Stand Up Paddling. Stand on a surfboard and paddle along using an oar. Apparently it's good for your 'core' muscles, because you're constantly using them while paddling. Supboarding can also be done at an easier level: Simply go a little slower or sit on your board. You can follow an introductory lesson, book organized tours or rent equipment at Windsurfing Curaçao at the Spanish Water.

(ⓢ) **Sup Curaçao (part of Windsurfing Curaçao)**
   Open: daily 10AM to 5:30PM | Address: Caracasbaai Peninsula, at the Spanish Water at Windsurfing Curaçao
   Supcuracao.com | Tel.: +599 9 738 0883 / +599 9 524 4974

Sailing or rent a motorboat

You can rent a sailboat, with or without a skipper at Sail Adventure Curaçao at the Spanish Water. If you want to sail yourself, you have to be in possession of a boat license. Always wanted to learn how to sail? You've come to the right place for sailing lessons on the coast of Curaçao. In addition, you can also go on a motorboat, dinghy or kayak. It's wonderful to spend some hours at the Spanish Water with your boat. There's a pier by the beach where you can moor at the nearby Santa Barbara Beach resort.

Sail Adventure Curaçao
Open: Wed till Sun 9AM to 6PM | Sailadventurecuracao.com | Tel.: +599 9 513 1604 / 767 2233

Boat trips Klein Curaçao

About six miles south of Curaçao is the mere 0.66 square miles, uninhabited island of Klein ('Little') Curaçao. Previously, this island was used to separate the healthy slaves from the sick slaves during the time of the slave trade before they were brought ashore to Curaçao. The sick slaves were quarantined on Klein Curaçao in the designated quarantine building, the remains of which can still be seen.

Today, Klein Curaçao is known as an idyllic paradise bounty island with a limited number of sights including a lighthouse and a shipwreck. Snorkeling off the coast of Klein Curaçao guarantees breathtaking images of the underwater world, with a reasonable chance of spotting a sea turtle.

You can find organizations that offer boat trips to Klein Curaçao everywhere on the island. You can also opt for 'super-fast', with a powerboat, see Powerboat Caribbean for more info.

Boat trips along the coast of Curaçao

There are several boat trips that sail along the coast of Curaçao. If you like snorkeling, you can choose to go on a snorkeling trip. Sail along the coast for a bit, after which the boat anchors at beautiful snorkeling spots so that everyone can go in the water. Want to go on a romantic tour? Then a 'sunset trip' might be an option for you.

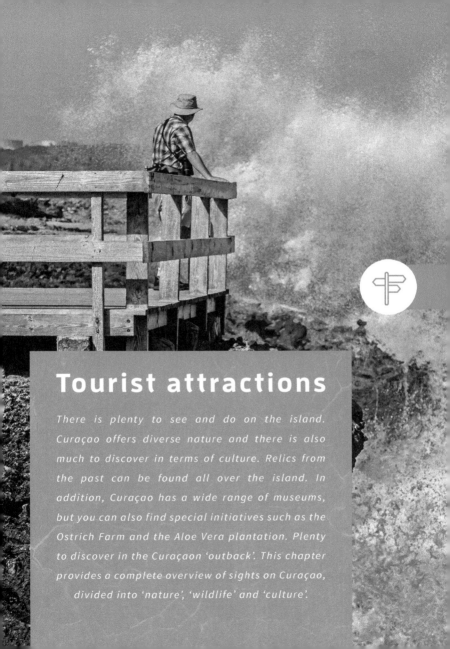

Tourist attractions

There is plenty to see and do on the island. Curaçao offers diverse nature and there is also much to discover in terms of culture. Relics from the past can be found all over the island. In addition, Curaçao has a wide range of museums, but you can also find special initiatives such as the Ostrich Farm and the Aloe Vera plantation. Plenty to discover in the Curaçaon 'outback'. This chapter provides a complete overview of sights on Curaçao, divided into 'nature', 'wildlife' and 'culture'.

KAS DI PAL'I MAÏSHI
(CUNUCU-HOUSE)

CHRISTOFFELPARK

SHETE BOKA PARK

Westpunt

CHRISTOFFEL
PARK

Lagun

Jan Donker

Barber

Soto

Weg naar Santa Cruz

LANDHUIS KNIP

Tera
Korá

Weg naar Westpunt

HATO

Sint
Willibrordus

Jan
Kok

Grote Berg

Weg naar Westpunt

Jan Kok Baai

Bullenbaai

Weg naar Bullenbaai

LANDHUIS GROOT
SANTA MARTHA

Sint
Michiel

NENA SANCHEZ
LANDHUIS JAN KOK

Blauwbaai

GALLERY ALMA BLOU

THE CURAÇAON MUSEUM

KURÁ HULANDA MUSEUM

 NATURE

 **MUSEUMS**

 MANSIONS

 WILDLIFE

 ART GALLERIES

Overview of tourist attractions on Curaçao

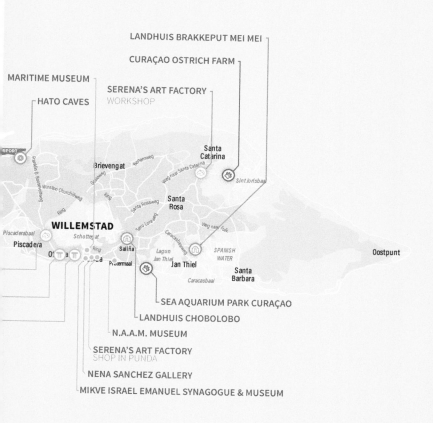

LANDHUIS BRAKKEPUT MEI MEI

CURAÇAO OSTRICH FARM

MARITIME MUSEUM

SERENA'S ART FACTORY
WORKSHOP

HATO CAVES

Santa
Catarina

RPORT

Franklin D. Rooseveltweg

Brievengat

Rooharmweg

Winston Churchillweg

Gosieweg

Weg naar Santa Catalina

Sint Jorisbaai

Ring

Santa
Rosa

Santa Rosaweg

Ring

WILLEMSTAD

Piscaderabaai

Schottegat

Piscadera

Saru Loraweg

Weg naar Fuik

Caracasbaaiweg

O...a

Saliña

Lagun

SPANISH
WATER

Oostpunt

Jan Thiel

Pietermaai

Jan Thiel

Santa
Barbara

Caracasbaai

SEA AQUARIUM PARK CURAÇAO

LANDHUIS CHOBOLOBO

N.A.A.M. MUSEUM

SERENA'S ART FACTORY
SHOP IN PUNDA

NENA SANCHEZ GALLERY

MIKVE ISRAEL EMANUEL SYNAGOGUE & MUSEUM

Nature

As mentioned previously, the nature on this small island is quite diverse. The rugged north coast, the idyllic bays in the south, the green hills of the Christoffel Park and the vast salt pans, places that always show a different side of the island. Below you'll find a selection of the most beautiful nature sights Curaçao has to offer.

Christoffel park

The national park Christoffel park is a must during your stay on Curaçao. Many different tropical plant and animal species can be found here. Think of colorful birdlife, deer and lizards and wild orchids, cacti and local tree species, such as dividivis and acacias. The CARMABI Foundation is committed to maintaining and protecting this beautiful stretch of nature. The foundation provides all sorts of activities to explore the park.

WALKING

The park offers eight hiking routes, varying in length and difficulty. You can explore this on your own or book a guide. A guide is experienced in spotting wild animals and they can tell you stories and facts that only the locals know about. At the entrance, in the store, you can get a map that shows the routes and information about the flora, fauna and historical locations in the park.

tip! CHRISTOFFEL MOUNTAIN

The steep climb to the top of the 1200-feet-high Christoffel Mountain is perhaps the most extraordinary hike on Curaçao. Every fit person can join this climb, provided you can handle the enormous heights and steep cliffs. The route goes across sandy and rocky paths and over tree stumps. But the view on top of the summit is more than worth the adventurous climb. Especially when the sky is clear, you can look over the entire island and the endless Caribbean Sea that stretches beyond.

It's a good idea to start the climb before 9am. Due to the heat and intensity of the climb, departure later than 10am is not allowed. Do not forget to exchange your flip flops for sturdy shoes and bring enough water.

JEEP SAFARI

You can explore the park by car, as there is a paved road that goes through the park. You can also join a safari tour: a guide will lead you through the highlights of the park with an open jeep and talk about the nature and history of the park and Curaçao. There are tours of two and four hours. It's also possible to explore the park by bicycle.

SAVONET MUSEUM

In the heart of Christoffel Park is the former Savonet Plantation. The mansion and out-buildings have been completely restored and converted into a museum. The museum provides insight into the history of the park and its inhabitants. From the life of the Arawak Indians who lived here 4,000 years ago, to life during the slavery period, ending with life in the park today. Both the cultural and natural developments in the park are highlighted. For recent admission prices go to Savonetmuseum.org. See opening times for the park below.

Christoffel park

Daily 7:30AM - 2PM (access untill 1:30PM) | Entrance park at Savonet (at the side of the Weg naar Westpunt) Fees Christoffel Park + FREE entrance to Savonet Museum: Adults $14.50, children 6 - 12 years $4.50, children <6 years free. Group fee: $8.50 p.p. (at least 15 people) | Website: Christoffelpark.org | Tel.: +599 9 864 0363

Shete Boka Park

Right next to Christoffel Park, on the northwest coast of the island is the Shete Boka Park. Literally translated, 'shete boka' means 'seven inlets'. This national park was established in 1994 and is also protected by the CARMABI foundation. On the Weg naar Westpunt, towards Westpunt, and past the Christoffel Park you'll find the entrance to Shete Boka Park. Do not expect green, lush hills, but rather a rugged lunar landscape, where the winds are a bit stronger and the sea hits the shoreline. This coastline contains the seven deep inlets.

CAVE AND BREEDING GROUND

From inland it's not that noticeable, but when you walk down the stone stairs at Boka Tabla (the centrally located boka in the extension of the parking lot) and enter the cave, the waves rush in and hit the rocks. In normal weather conditions it is safe to enter the cave, but it's always at your own risk. There is also a warning sign. Fun fact: The bokas are a protected breeding ground for sea turtles. Unfortunately these are not visible during a walk along the bokas.

HIKES

You can drive along the coastline by car and visit all bokas. If you have more time, you can explore (parts of) the park on foot. Two walking routes have been mapped out:

1. A one-hour walk to Boka Wandomi. Boka Wandomi is a natural bridge that has been carved into the rocks by the water.

2. A one-hour walk that leads past Boka Brown (one of the breeding grounds for sea turtles) and Boka Pistol, the boka where the water hits the cove at its most powerful. The boka pushes up the water explosively, which sounds like a gunshot.

When hiking, keep in mind that there is no shade in the Shete Boka Park. The strong wind means you also notice the bright sun less. So make sure to put on plenty of sunscreen. A hat or scarf to cover your head is also not a bad idea here. Finally, wearing sturdy shoes is also recommended. The landscape gets quite rocky.

ⓘ **Shete Boka Park**
Daily 9AM - 4PM | Address: Weg naar Westpunt | Entrance fee: $10 p.p., you can get a map at the entrance

Caves of Hato

Near the airport are the Caves of Hato. Remains of Curaçao's first civilization, the Arawak Indians, can be found here. They lived in these caves. The mural drawings that are still vaguely visible are proof of this. In addition, skeletons have been found of these first inhabitants.

Many centuries later, slaves fled to these caves to hide from their slave drivers. The burning torches left visible traces of soot in the caves. Nowadays the caves are inhabited by bats.

The caves can be visited during a tour with a guide. The guide will lead you through the different 'rooms' with impressive stalactite formations and tell you about the history of the caves.

ⓘ **Caves of Hato**
   Daily 9AM - 4PM | Address: F.D. Rooseveltweg z/n | Multilingual tours start every hour, final tour starts at 4PM
   (tour is compulsory) | Entrance fee: >12 years $9, children <13 years $7

Wildlife

Many small animals live in the wild in Curaçao, such as (predatory) birds, flamingos, deer and iguanas. Curaçao is also rich with underwater fauna, with reef fish, turtles, rays and dolphins. Wildlife spotting is great at the Christoffel Park. In addition, there are some places where animals are kept.

Sea Aquarium Park Curaçao

CURACAO SEA AQUARIUM

Bordering Mambo Beach Boulevard is the Sea Aquarium Park Curaçao, which consists of several parts. One of them is the Curaçao Sea Aquarium, an 'aquarium park' with 46 different aquariums. These are constantly supplied with fresh seawater using a unique open system. The Sea Aquarium houses all kinds of reef fish and predators, such as stingrays and sharks.

In the outdoor area there are several lagoons with sea turtles, sea lions, sharks, stingrays and dolphins. Educational sessions are regularly held here with sea lions and dolphins. The dolphin demonstration in particular is a very popular feature here. The Curaçao Sea Aquarium regularly provides care and shelter for injured or rejected animals.

DOLPHIN ACADEMY

At Dolphin Academy you can swim with dolphins. There are several 'encounters' available to book: from touching dolphins in a basin to snorkeling and diving with dolphins in the open sea. It is advisable to book an 'encounter' in time. For more information, visit dolphin-academy.com.

CURAÇAO DOLPHIN THERAPY AND RESEARCH CENTER (CDTC)

The CDTC offers a unique and effective therapy program for people suffering from, for example, autism, Down syndrome and mental illnesses such as depression, PTSD and burnout. This is provided by qualified therapists in collaboration with dolphins, in an inviting Caribbean environment. For more information, visit the website of Curaçao Dolphin Therapy center, cdtc.info.

CURASUB

A very special excursion is a descent into the deep sea with a five-person submarine, the Curasub. Without getting wet you descend to 1,000 feet into the sea to explore places no diver has yet been. An excursion with the Curasub does not require training and is suitable for a wide audience, because the conditions remain the same above water. There are several trips you can book. Go to substation-curacao.com for more information and reservations.

At the adjacent diving school, Ocean Encounters, you can book a so-called 'Animal Encounter' where you can view several sea animals up close. Equipped with snorkeling or diving equipment you can view and feed sharks, stingrays and other large fish in one of the Curaçao Sea Aquarium's lagoons. Access to the Sea Aquarium Park is included in an animal encounter.

ⓘ **Sea Aquarium Park Curaçao**
Daily 8AM - 5PM | Address Bapor Kibra z/n | Adults: $ 21, children 5 - 12 years $ 11, under 5 years free, 60+ $ 11
Website: sea-aquarium-park.com | Tel.: +599 9 461 6666

Curaçao Ostrich Farm

A special initiative on the island is the Ostrich Farm. Once established as an export site where the eggs, chicks and meat of ostriches were exported to countries in South America. Since 1995, the farm has been open to visitors and there are several excursions you can book, you can eat ostrich steak in Zambezi restaurant and buy African souvenirs in the souvenir store.

Book a safari tour to learn all about the ostrich and the farm. With a bus you make a tour of the terrain and an enthusiastic guide will tell you lots about the life of the ostriches on the farm. This is accompanied by interactions with the ostriches: you can feed the birds, touch eggs to feel their hard shell and with a bit of luck hold an ostrich chick just hatched from the egg.

For some time now there have also been quad tours at the Ostrich Farm to explore the bordering Sint Jorisbaai.

After such an extensive tour it's great to just sit back and relax on the porch at the Zambezi restaurant. The menu includes a mix of international and Curaçaon cuisine with an African twist. In addition, Zambezi – as expected - serves a number of dishes containing ostrich meat. The ostrich steak is a must. Can't get enough of the ostrich? Buy an ostrich egg for at home or to make a delicious omelet. Drill a hole in the shell so you don't break the whole egg, so it can still serve as a showpiece at home. Dining is only possible on Fridays, but you must reserve.

ⓘ **Curaçao Ostrich Farm & Restaurant Zambezi**
Daily 9AM - 4:30PM, tours daily 9AM - 4PM (every hour) | Address: Groot St. Joris West | Adults $ 17, children $ 14 | Website: curacaoostrichfarm.com | Tel.: +599 9 747 2777

Culture

Curaçao offers a wide range of museums. Many museums tell you something about the history of the island. A number of old plantation houses have been converted into museums. But there are also art galleries, a Jewish museum and the Maritime Museum. In short, Curaçao also has plenty to offer when it comes to culture. Enjoy a selection of museums, art galleries and mansions on the island.

Museums

THE CURAÇAO MUSEUM

This museum is located in a former military hospital in Otrobanda. The museum has been home to collections of objects from the 18th , 19th, 20th and 21st century since 1948. The collection consists mainly of furniture, paintings by local and international painters and sculptures. There's also a SNIP cockpit on display, the first KLM aircraft to cross the ocean, from the Netherlands to Curaçao. The museum mainly provides an overview of how people used to live on the island.

ⓘ **The Curaçao Museum**
Tue - Fri 8:30AM - 4:30PM, Sat 10AM - 4PM | Address: Van Leeuwenhoekstraat, Otrobanda | Adults: NAF 11.50, children 6 - 11 years NAF 5.75 | Website: thecuracaomuseum.com | Tel.: +599 9 462 3873

MARITIME MUSEUM

The maritime history of Curaçao goes back more than 500 years. The museum begins with the story of the voyages of discovery from European and Dutch colonization. Maritime history is described based on old nautical maps, ship models, navigation equipment and image and audio. The interior even resembles an old ship deck complete with railings, masts and deck boards. Both early and recent port history is discussed, with the ports of Curaçao serving as a transit port, oil refinery site and cruise ship berth. Finally, the port life of the Dutch Navy, which has a base here, is also discussed extensively. The museum offers various tours, including a tour of the port itself. The Maritime Museum gives a complete and lively picture of the port history of Curaçao.

ⓘ **Maritime Museum**
Mon - Sat 9AM - 4PM, sometimes on Sun (Nov - Apr, when there's a cruise ship)
Address: N. Van Den Brandhofstraat 1, Willemstad (Scharloo, opposite the floating market)
Full rate $7, children 6 - 11 years $3.50, children <6 years old free
Website: curacaomaritime.com | Tel.: +599 9 465 2327

NAAM - NATIONAL ARCHAEOLOGICAL AND ANTHROPOLOGICAL MUSEUM

This museum exhibits a large collection of archaeological and anthropological artifacts, dating from pre-colonial times up to the 20th century. You'll come across objects from the period of the slave trade, maritime objects and all kinds of other items, including crockery and jewelry, but also musical instruments and school material from a later period. Furthermore NAAM is dedicated to spreading knowledge about cultural history and strengthening cultural identity on the Dutch Antillian islands.

ⓘ **NAAM - Nationaal Archeologisch en Antropologisch Museum**
Mon - Fri 9AM - 12PM & 2PM - 5PM | Address: Johan van Walbeeckplein 13, Willemstad (Pietermaai)
Free entrance | Website: naam.cw | Tel.: +599 9 462 1933 / 34

JEWISH CULTURE HISTORICAL MUSEUM & MIKVE ISRAEL-EMANUEL SYNAGOGUE

This museum is part of the Mikve Israel-Emanuel Synagogue, the oldest synagogue in the Western Hemisphere that has remained in continuous use. The museum is located in the former living area and bath house of the rabbi. There's a patio located in the center of the museum. The museum and the synagogue have been thoroughly restored and many authentic colonial elements have also been restored. 17th- and 18th-century wealth is still evident. The museum houses replicas of engraved tombstones and various ceremonial and cultural objects, such as a Torah (first and most important part of the Jewish Bible), silverware and jewelry.

The synagogue itself contains mahogany furniture, antique brass chandeliers - in which real candles illuminate the synagogue - and the floor is covered with sand, symbolizing the Jewish journey through the desert. A handy bonus in earlier times was that the sand silenced the sound of the services that were being held in secret.

ⓘ Jewish Culture Historical Museum & Synagoge
Mon - Fri 9AM - 4:30PM | Services: Fri 7:30PM & Sat 10AM (appr. clothing required) | Address: Hanchi Snoa 29, (Punda) | Entrance fee: 'a small donation' | Website: snoa.com | Tel.: +599 9 461 1067

KURÀ HULANDA MUSEUM

This is the museum to go to in Curaçao when you want to learn more about the turbulent period that involved the slave trade between the Netherlands and Curaçao. The Kurà Hulanda Museum is an anthropological museum that gives a detailed picture of what happened to Curaçao during the time of slavery. In addition, the museum houses an extensive collection of African and Antillean (religious) art.

The museum is located in the middle of the Kurà Hulanda area. This site has been completely restored to its original state. The old laborer's houses have been converted into hotel rooms and arranged in a picturesque manner around a courtyard, where you'll regularly hear live music being played. After a visit to the museum you can also enjoy a great lunch here. In order to better understand the history and contemporary life of Curaçao and the Caribbean, this museum is an absolute *must*.

ⓘ Kurà Hulanda Museum
Mon - Sat 9:30AM - 4:30PM | Address: Klipstraat 9, Willemstad (Otrobanda) | Adults $10, children up to 12 years $7, students $8 | Website: kurahulanda.com | Tel.: +599 9 434 7700

KAS DI PAL'I MAÏSHI (CUNUCU HOUSE)

Just after slavery was abolished, former slaves built their own shelters in the countryside: the 'cunucu' of Curaçao. The houses were built from the materials that were available at the time: a roof of corn stalks, walls of limestone. Kas di pal'i maïshi therefore means 'house of corn stalks'. Until about 1950 many Curaçaoans lived in this way. Today, only a few of the cunucu houses can be found on the island. The Kas di Pal'i Maïshi Museum is a cunucu cottage restored by the Monument preservation organization, where you can learn more about how Curaçaoans used to live here in the countryside.

ⓘ Kas di Pal'i Maïshi (cunucu house)
Tue - Sun 10AM - 2PM | Address: Dokterstuin 27, Weg naar Westpunt | Tel.: +599 9 666 9973

Art galleries

NENA SANCHEZ

Bright colors, mystical blue women and iconic images of Curaçao are the hallmarks of Nena Sanchez. Nena Sanchez was able to reproduce the colorful Curaçao in her paintings like no other. Her love for the island where she was born and raised is therefore reflected in every artwork she produced. Her paintings can be admired in her gallery and atelier in the Jan Kok mansion and in her gallery in Punda. But you can also view her artworks in the street in the form of murals.

On 18 August 2017, Nena Sanchez died at the age of 73. Her art, fortunately, can still be admired at the locations listed below.

Nena Sanchez - Jan Kok mansion
Tue - Sat 10AM - 5PM | Address: Weg naar Sint Willibrordus (direction Westpunt)
Tel.: +599 9 738 2377 / 864 0965

Nena Sanchez - gallery in Punda
Tue - Fri 10AM - 5PM | Address: Windstraat 15, Willemstad (Punda)
Website: nenasanchez.com | Tel.: +599 9 461 2882

CHICHI SCULPTURES

Chichi sculptures are figurines of Curaçao women who are known as the 'big sisters' in their community. A 'big sister' in Curaçao is a caring person that you can always count on. The Chichi figurines were created by Serena Israel, a German artist who emigrated to Curaçao. The big sisters inspired her and the Chichi was born. Because the demand for Chichis grew steadily, she called in the help of local women to manufacture the Chichis with her. More than 50 women paint Chichis for Serena. You can find out which woman made your Chichi via the number on the Chichi you purchased. Today, Serena Israel manufactures and sells the sculptures in Serena's Art Factory. She also gives workshops, in which you can paint your own Chichi. The Chichis are also for sale at Serena's souvenir store in Punda.

Serena's Art Factory - **Workshop**
Mon - Sat 9AM - 5PM | Address: Jan Luis 87A (on the road to the Ostrich Farm)
Free entrance | Tel. +599 9 738 0648 | Workshops on appointment

Serena's Art Factory - **Store punda**
Mon - Sat 10AM - 5PM | Address: Windstraat, Gomezplein Willemstad (Punda) | Chichi-curacao.com

ALMA BLOU GALLERY

Alma Blou - 'blue soul' in Papiamento - is a gallery located in Habaai mansion. Habaai mansion is known as one of the most beautiful mansions on Curaçao. It used to be a popular accommodation spot for wealthy families and officers on the island. The gallery exhibits an extensive collection of artwork by local and Caribbean artists. You can buy exclusive souvenirs to your heart's content in the gallery shop. The mansion also has a large sculpture garden where you can relax and enjoy the artwork on show.

Galerie Alma Blou
Tue - Fri 9:30AM - 5:30PM, Sat 10AM - 2PM | Address: Frater Radulphusweg 4, Willemstad (Habaai)
Free entrance | Website: galleryalmablou.com | Tel.: +599 9 462 8896

Mansions

After the West India Company could no longer maintain power over the land on the island, plots of land were sold to private individuals. The brand new largescale landowners had impressive mansions built on their land.

Mansion means 'Landhuis' in Dutch. All over Curaçao you can recognise mansions by the word 'Landhuis' in their names.

ACHITECTURE

The tropical climate was taken into account in the layout of the houses. Each mansion had at least one spacious veranda, the bedroom was on the cool side and the kitchen on the wind side of the house. No expense was spared to make the house as luxurious as possible. Slaves were purchased and appointed as domestic help, clerks or plantation workers. Smaller houses were built around the mansions where the slaves stayed.

LOCATION

Initially the mansions were mainly built around the central Schottegat, close to the port of Curaçao. Later on, mansions were also built on other parts of the island, between the plantations. The plantation slaves had a terrible existence, in exchange for a minimal salary and 'lodging' they worked the entire days in extremely tough conditions on the plantation fields.

Many of the mansions fell into disrepair in the last century, but luckily many of them have also been given a new destination. The architectural delights and chic ornaments have been restored. With the restoration of the mansions, the painful memories of the past also remained alive. We have made a selected list of mansions that are definitely worth visiting.

The original name of this mansion is 'Zoutpan' ('Salt pan'). The land around Chobolobo was formerly the place where salt was acquired. Because salt was scarce, and therefore costly, it was an important source of income on the downwind islands. At the end of the 18th century the name of the mansion was changed to 'Sebollobo', the meaning of which is still unknown. It is suspected that it's an Indian name.

Blue Curacao

In 1946, this mansion was known worldwide for its liqueur distillery. In the Second World War liqueurs were very popular as alcoholic beverages, because the beer was of poor quality during that time. Chobolobo is still the distillery for the world famous liqueur Blue Curaçao. On Chobolobo you can take a look in the kitchen at the distillery and, of course, sample this sky blue drink. You can explore Chobolobo on your own or take a guided tour. Finally, enjoy a great lunch, taste the home-made ice cream or drink cocktails in the bar after a tour.

Landhuis Chobolobo
Mon - Fri 8AM - 5PM | Address: Elias R.A. Moreno Boulevard, Willemstad (Salina)
Free entrance | Tours and tasting from $ 12.50 | Website: chobolobo.com | Tel.: +599 9 461 3526

LANDHUIS GROOT SANTA MARTHA

Near the village of Soto, in the direction of Westpunt, is the mansion known as Groot Santa Martha. This is one of the oldest mansions on Curaçao, built at the end of the 17th century. Until 1825, it was mainly used for cultivating sugar, which was used to make, among other things, rum. After 1825 the mansion was focused on salt production. At the end of the 19th century, 90 percent of the salt in Curaçao came from the bay near Santa Martha.

Sheltered Workshop

This mansion is still in good condition due to the many restorations it has undergone. It is a stately mansion built in colonial style. Today it's owned by the government, who set up a shelter and treatment center for physically and/or mentally disabled people there. The residents can develop themselves in certain crafts, such as carpentry, basket weaving or maintaining the livestock on the site. The products they make are offered for sale on the premises. The institution behind this, Fundashon Tayer Soshal, ensures that people with a disability learn a trade and become part of society.

Vast farmlands

The plot of land around Santa Martha is vast and opulent. The typical vegetation specific to Curaçao grows and blooms in abundance here and there are many birds and animals to spot. Furthermore, livestock is kept here and there's also an orchard and a vegetable garden. All available to view for a walk, with or without a guided tour. You can also explore the terrain on horseback. Make an appointment using the contact information below. Since 2012, a permanent exhibition of archaeological and anthropological objects has been exhibited in the mansion. Finally, there is a cafeteria where the residents provide you with drinks, snacks, breakfast or lunch.

ⓘ **Landhuis Groot Santa Martha**
Mon - Fri 9AM - 4PM | Address: Landhuis Groot Santa Martha z/n, Soto | Website: tayersoshal.com | Tel.: +599 9 864 1323

LANDHUIS KNIP

Perched on top of the green hills to the west is Landhuis Knip, also known as Kenepa, named after the fruit from the kenepa tree. It was once one of the most prosperous mansions, Dividivi seed pots and sheep wool were produced here. Knip Mansion is not only worth a visit for its location, but also for its history. On 17 August 1795, the largest slave revolt of the Caribbean started here.

Led by Tula, a few of the more than 350 slaves who worked at Knip refused to work. They moved eastwards across the island and more and more slaves joined the demonstration. Near Santa Cruz, they encountered an army of police and the uprising was crushed by force. The leaders of the uprising were sentenced to death. To this day, Tula symbolizes the freedom struggle and is extremely important to Curaçaoans.

The Tula museum is now housed in the mansion, where an exhibition about the life of slaves on the island and an exhibition of antique furniture can be seen. Besides the Kurá Hulanda, the Knip mansion is well worth a visit to learn about the former life of the slaves on the island.

ⓘ **Landhuis Knip**
Tue - Fri 11:30AM - 4PM, Sun 10:30AM - 5:30PM | Address: side street of Weg naar Santa Cruz, dir. Westpunt | 'Small' Entrance fee | Tel.: +599 9 888 6396

OTHER MANSIONS

Many of the other mansions are now operated as catering establishments. *Landhuis Brakkeput Mei Mei* is a good example. Great grill dishes are served out on the spacious terrace. Enjoy your food in the open air under large trees filled with twinkling lights. In addition regular band and salsa nights are organized here. This mansion is located near the Spanish Water on the east side of the island.

Landhuis Dokterstuin is the place to be for good local food. The on-site Komedor Krioyo restaurant serves authentic Creole cuisine in the cozy courtyard garden.

Shopping

Spilt a glass of red wine on that beautiful summer dress, or is it time for a new swimsuit? No worries! There are several shopping malls scattered around Curaçao where you'll be able to find everything you need. The following is an overview of the largest shopping malls on the island.

Overview of shopping locations on Curaçao

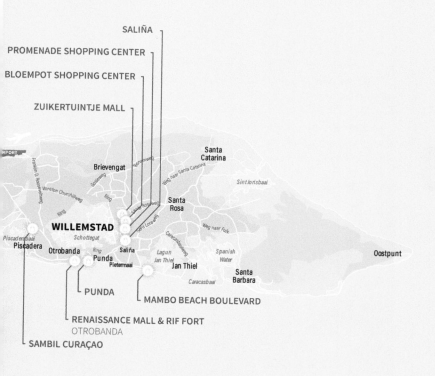

SALIÑA

PROMENADE SHOPPING CENTER

BLOEMPOT SHOPPING CENTER

ZUIKERTUINTJE MALL

Santa
Catarina

Brievengat

Sint Jorisbaai

Santa
Rosa

WILLEMSTAD

Schottegat

Weg naar Fuik

Piscaderabaai

Oostpunt

Piscadera

Otrobanda

Saliña

Spanish
Water

Punda

Lagun
Jan Thiel

Pietermaai

Jan Thiel

Santa
Barbara

Caracasbaai

PUNDA

MAMBO BEACH BOULEVARD

RENAISSANCE MALL & RIF FORT
OTROBANDA

SAMBIL CURAÇAO

Wide range

Because Curaçao is the largest transit port in the Caribbean, there are all sorts of things available for sale on the island. This is evident in the diverse range of stores on display.

In general, all stores open from eight in the morning to six in the evening: at noon they close for two hours. The catering establishments remain open. Besides Willemstad, there are a number of other nice shopping malls in the area.

Otrobanda

Until recently Punda was the district in Willemstad with the nicest and largest number of stores. Since the Renaissance Mall & Rif Fort opened in Otrobanda in 2009, including a luxury shopping street just outside the riffort, Otrobanda has also become interesting for fanatical shoppers. You can go here for, among other things, designer labels and jewelry. In addition, there is also an art gallery where exhibitions are regularly held with works mainly from Curaçao and the Caribbean, but also from other parts of the world.

Punda

As far back as the 17th century, Punda was already the trading hub of Curaçao. The first streets on the island were built here, right at the entrance to the seaport. The warehouses along the Handelskade show how important this part of the island was for trade. The shopping streets in Punda are perfect for a nice stroll. The range of stores is quite large although the same is often available in those stores. There are various electronics stores that all sell the latest phones, televisions and computer equipment.

Apart from electronics, there is plenty to be had in terms of perfumes and cosmetics. In the famous Penha building, on the corner near the pontoon bridge, a wide range of cosmetic products from well-known brands are on offer and the store windows of the various jewelers are filled with jewelry. The big name clothing brands are also represented.

Finally, there are also plenty of gift stores to be found here and items are also sold on the street. Key rings, towels and inexpensive clothing are distributed through many stores in Punda.

Shopping malls

Sambil

Sambil is a giant, hypermodern shopping mall that is fully covered and AC cooled. Originally, Sambil was a South American concept, with shopping malls in different countries. This complex was opened in Curaçao in 2015, with a wide variety of stores.

They even have many different clothing stores. Children can have fun under the supervision of an adult at the indoor playground Kidi's Park. They can also enjoy themselves on the trampolines at Zero Gravity. For the little ones there are several free play corners.

At the central food court you have a wide choice of fast food restaurants. Tired of shopping? Then visit the bowling alley, StrikeZone, or grab a movie in the most advanced cinema on the island CineMark.

Promenade Shopping center

With a central location on the island, about 1/2 mile from Saliña, is the Promenade Shopping center on the Schottegatweg-Oost. In this shopping center you can find stylish women's, men's and children's clothing brands. Shoes are imported from countries such as Spain, Italy and the Netherlands and jewelry and watches from Switzerland. In short, you can find everything you need in clothing and accessories right here, all under one roof. For a pit stop, go to Craving Sushi or the lunchroom De Dames.

Bloempot Shopping center

A thousand feet past the Promenade Shopping center you'll find the Bloempot Shopping center. This shopping center is spacious but the number of stores is limited. You can go here for clothes, shoes and jewelry and there are a few hair salons. Beauty treatments such as manicures and pedicures are also available here. On the large - covered - terrace at Delifrance you can enjoy a refreshing drink and/or lunch.

Zuikertuintje Mall

The adjacent Zuikertuintje Mall was thoroughly renovated a few years ago. It now consists mainly of branches that sell major clothing brands. It also has an optician and a book store. So if you've finished the books you brought with you, just go here for new reading material. Looking for more English books? Visit Mensing's Caminada book store at Schottegatweg-Oost.

Mambo Beach Boulevard

A brand new shopping center is located right by the beach of Mambo Beach. Here you'll find many clothing stores, a tattoo parlor, beauty stores, jewelers and gift stores. All stores are open seven days a week from early till late. Their motto? There's always something to do at Mambo Beach BLVD. In addition to stores, there are also many restaurants and cafés here, ranging from a traditional Dutch snackbar to a sushi restaurant and a Starbucks.

Snorkeling & diving

Curaçao originates from volcanic limestone on which coral has been deposited over many centuries. Off the coast of Curaçao are beautiful coral reefs, home to an array of flora and fauna. Brightly colored tropical fish, seahorses, sea turtles and barracudas are among the many inhabitants of the underwater world that surrounds Curaçao.

If you don't like diving, then a snorkeling set is also enough to enjoy the under water splendor.

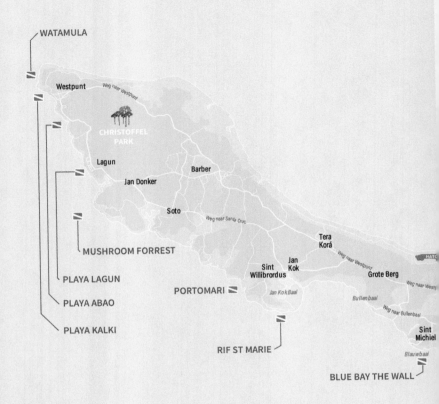

WATAMULA

Westpunt

Weg naar Westpunt

CHRISTOFFEL
PARK

Lagun

Barber

Jan Donker

Soto

Weg naar Santa Cruz

MUSHROOM FORREST

Tera
Korá

Weg naar Westpunt

PLAYA LAGUN

Jan
Kok

Sint
Willibrordus

Grote Berg

PLAYA ABAO

PORTOMARI

Jan Kok Baai

Weg naar Westp

Bullenbaai

Weg naar Bullenbaai

PLAYA KALKI

Sint
Michiel

RIF ST MARIE

Blauwbaai

BLUE BAY THE WALL

Overview of popular diving sites on Curaçao

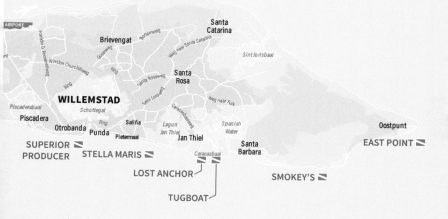

Snorkeling

If you go on vacation to Curaçao then a snorkeling set is one of the most important travel items you can have. There are several beaches where you can enjoy the beautiful tropical fish that live in the Caribbean Sea just feet from the coast. In addition, various snorkeling trips are organized to take you to well-known spots around the island.

Purchasing a snorkeling set: what to pay attention to

You can purchase a snorkeling set for a few bucks in one of the many diving stores on Curaçao. When fitting the mask (goggles) it is important that the mask closes properly and is sealed around the edges. You can easily test this by pushing the mask against your face without putting the strap around your head and then breathing in through your nose. If the mask fits properly, it should stay on your face without you holding it.

Snorkeling beaches

You can take out your snorkeling set on almost all the beaches that you come across from Willemstad towards Westpunt. There's always something to see underwater, anywhere around the island. For an overview of all beaches, see page 40 and further. We've highlighted a few beaches here that are ideal for snorkeling.

PORTOMARI

At PortoMari there are several reef balls in the water just a few feet from the coast. These concrete balls are teeming with tropical fish that you can observe closely with a snorkel.

PLAYA LAGUN AND PLAYA ABAO

At Playa Lagun and Playa Abao (Grote Knip), you can see beautiful fish along the rocks. If you swim a bit, you come to the drop-off, where the seabed slopes abruptly and the coral reef begins. It is really enjoyable here in clear waters and sunny weather! Beware, however, for boats and water scooters that, particularly in the weekends, often sail across the bay towards the beach.

PLAYA KALKI

On the beach of Playa Kalki, which has been nicknamed *Alice in Wonderland*, there are always divers present. There's also a diving store here. In addition to stunningly colorful fish, the mushroom-shaped coral formations are something to look forward to.

STELLA MARIS

To the east of Willemstad at Mambo Beach Boulevard is the Stella Maris reef. This special reef owes its name to a shipwreck that went missing, discovered at great depths not long ago by a team of divers. Because the wreck sank to such an enormous depth, it isn't visible to snorkelers and divers. Yet this place is worth exploring with your snorkel because of the reef behind the dividing rocks at Mambo Beach Boulevard. At some places in the rock formation there are passages through which you can get to the reef.

Snorkeling trips

There are many snorkeling trips on Curaçao, both at diving schools and on cruises around the island. Often you'll end up at the same snorkeling sites, so it's a smart idea to compare prices.

TUGBOAT

Many of these snorkeling trips lead to the familiar tugboat, undoubtedly the most beautiful snorkeling spot on the island. This tugboat that sank more than 30 years ago is only a few feet under water. The boat has been swallowed up by coral and plants that, in recent decades, formed a shelter for many tropical fish species. The boat and the fish around it provide fantastic photo opportunities, which would not be out of place on a postcard. Be careful, however, that you do not touch the boat, it is partly rusted and also covered with different types of coral that can cause irritation.

There's also plenty to see in the rock formations next to the tugboat. In the caverns in the rocks, you can often see moray eels, scorpion fish and crabs. You should not be surprised if you suddenly find yourself fishing between an entire school, that often swim with the current along the rock faces. You can also come here by car, see page 148.

Aquafari

One of the newest attractions on Curaçao is Aquafari. On a futuristic-looking underwater scooter, you float among the fish under the supervision of a professional diver. Ideal if you're unable to, or don't want to, go diving, but still want to explore the world underwater. For more information see Aquafari.net or visit Aquafari in Piscadera, next to Pirate Bay.

Diving

For real underwater enthusiasts there is only one option, of course, and that's with a tank on your back descending along the spectacular coral reefs that are scattered around

Curaçao. Also, or perhaps correctly, for those who have never been diving before, this is an excellent opportunity to get acquainted with the sport. The courses that are offered in Curaçao are generally of high quality and PADI certified. It is very pleasant to learn to dive in Curaçao in the warm water surrounded by tropical fish.

Introductory dive

A common phrase is: "diving is not for me". If you fall into that category, then it is really worth considering an introductory diving session, without obligation. This can be done for very little money at most recognized diving schools on the island. You don't descend far during the test dive, it is mainly about getting used to the equipment and moving around underwater. This way you can familiarize yourself with the sport and get a taste of the fascinating underwater world. Inquire at one of the many diving schools about the options available to you; who knows, you might just love it.

Diving courses

Diving courses are available at all levels, for beginners and advanced. During a beginners course, also called PADI open water course, the most important thing is to familiarize yourself with the diving equipment and to practice a lot of possible emergency situations under water. These exercises are of course done in a very controlled way and you learn what to do in the sea in certain situations.

You'll learn this partly in practice during the various dives you will go on with a small class of divers, but a large part of it is theory. Before you can complete the course you must first take an exam. All in all, the course lasts about three days. Once you've successfully completed them - and practice shows that the success rate is pretty much 100% - you are authorized to hire diving equipment all over the world and start diving. The only limitation is that you may 'only' dive to a depth of 60 feet.

You can also follow advanced courses. Here you dive to a depth of about 100 feet and there are opportunities to go boat diving, diving for wreckages and/or night diving. This is not only about the art of diving, but also about diving more adventurously and more actively.

Buddy

In diving, there is one restriction that always applies: you are never allowed to go diving on your own. From the basic course you will learn to dive with a buddy. A buddy is your underwater partner, and you should always keep an eye on each other. During the course you will also learn how to communicate with your buddy under water, and how you can help each other in an emergency situation. Are you the only diver in your travel group? Then contact one of the diving schools on the island, often they form buddy teams during boat trips or a supervised dive.

The most beautiful diving locations
If you have your diving license, then nothing stands in the way of jumping into the deep. Every diving school on Curaçao has a varied range of guided dives, but also possibilities to rent equipment and to dive independently (with buddy).

On the following pages you will find a selection of diving locations around the island that are recommended by experienced divers as the most beautiful locations.

West of Willemstad

WATA MULA
This is the northernmost diving spot on Curaçao, with a rugged and authentic underwater world. The flora and fauna at Wata Mula are truly spectacular and unique. There is also an underwater cave. There are large walls at the bottom and occasionally sharks and turtles can be seen here.

PLAYA KALKI

Playa Kalki is located near Westpunt and is the perfect place for sun lovers, divers and snorkelers. Kalki means limestone in Papiamento and refers to the limestone in the cliffs. In general, the waves are calm and the current is weak. The beach consists of sand and is covered with different types of hard coral. There are morays, crabs, mushroom-shaped coral formations and multicolored reef fish. When you reach 100 feet or deeper you discover large areas where table and leaf coral live.

MUSHROOM FOREST

Mushroom Forest owes its name to the enormous forest of mushroom-shaped coral formations. Many fish and other sea animals find shelter between these giant formations. Mushroom Forest is therefore a unique diving spot. It's best to go to Mushroom Forest by boat, because it is quite far from the beach of Playa Lagun. In addition, the existing cliffs don't make it easy to access Mushroom Forest. You can book a boat trip to this amazing diving spot, through various different diving schools.

PORTOMARI

PortoMari is also a beautiful and unique diving spot on Curaçao because of the many fish and the double reef, which is easily accessible here. It's also because of the double reef and the valley in between that it's known as The Valley. PortoMari has a flat sandy bottom and you can see rare fish such as pairs of cornet fish and sometimes small nurse sharks and eagle rays. Other reef fish that you can see include squid, angel and parrotfish, groupers, yellowtail snappers, trumpet fish and stingrays.

SUPERIOR PRODUCER

The Superior Producer is an overgrown wreckage that lies at a depth of more than 100 feet, just outside the entrance of St. Anna Bay. In 1977 the ship sailed out of the harbor, on the way to Isla Margarita, when it let in water. The ship was unfortunately no longer salvageable. It was then dragged out of the harbor and allowed to sink. After all these years the ship has been completely swallowed up by coral, and you can see several reef fish, barracudas, groupers, corals and anemones here.

From Willemstad you follow the road along the coast in a westerly direction and parallel to the Aqualectra factory, follow the signs for Double reef. A supervised dive is recommended, because it is quite difficult to determine the exact position of the ship and the current can be treacherous.

East of Willemstad

EAST POINT

East Point or Oostpunt is, as the name suggests, located on the easternmost point of the island. This diving spot can only be reached by boat. There is a naturally formed underwater bridge of coral. Sharks, barracudas, eagle rays and sea turtles can regularly be spotted here.

LOST ANCHOR

This diving site is characterized by a particularly bright and colorful environment and a lushly vegetated drop-off. On the seabed there is an anchor that is now completely overgrown with coral, hence the name of this site. There are also many seahorses to see here.

SMOKEY'S

After a boat trip of about 20 minutes from Mambo Beach Boulevard, you'll arrive at this unique diving spot. The underwater world here is characterized by clear water that offers perfect views. Sharks and stingrays are regularly seen at this spot.

Restaurants

Because Curaçao is relatively close to the equator, the sun goes down pretty early. On average, it gets dark at seven o'clock in the evening in Curaçao. What could be better than to enjoy a refreshing drink at the end of the afternoon and see the sun set during a romantic dinner. In this chapter you'll find an independent selection of the many restaurants that Curaçao has to offer.

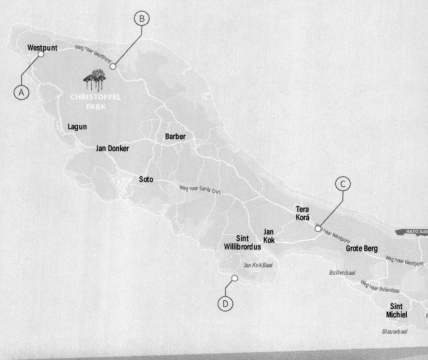

Westpunt

Weg naar Westpunt

CHRISTOFFEL PARK

Lagun

Jan Donker

Barber

Soto

Weg naar Santa Cruz

Tera Korá

Sint Willibrordus

Jan Kok

Jan Kok Baai

Grote Berg

Weg naar Westpunt

HATO AIRF

Weg naar Westpunt

Bullenbaai

Weg naar Bullenbaai

Sint Michiel

Blauwbaai

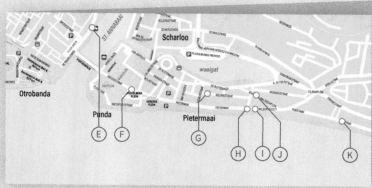

Otrobanda

ST. ANNABAAI

Scharloo

PLASA MUNDO MERCED

Waaigat

A. DE VEER STRAAT

WILHELMINA PLEIN

HENDRIK PLEIN

Punda

Pietermaai

Overview of restaurants on Curaçao

See a list of restaurants on page 109

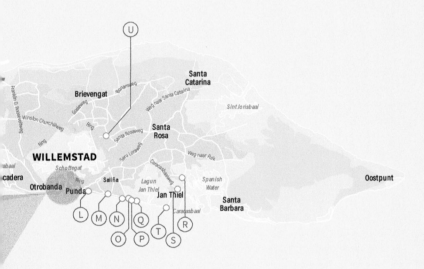

Restaurants on Curaçao

Curaçao has more than 300 restaurants, which are spread over the island. Most are located in or near Willemstad and at the popular beaches east of Willemstad. The price level doesn't differ that much from major cities in the USA and western Europe; a main course costs around USD 20.

In general, the restaurants on Curaçao are rated very highly. The fierce competition on the island means they have to deliver quality. At most restaurants, the nine-percent sales tax is included in the price. Some restaurants also include the tip in the price, which is specified in the menu.

Traditional Cuisine

The original Curaçaon cuisine is unique in the world. Just like the population, the Curaçao kitchen originated from many different cultures and influences. Unique to Curaçao are the pastchi (patties) and stoba (stewed meat). Many dishes are also served with pica, a spicy pepper sauce. Since Curaçao is an island, meals often include fish in some form or other.

Places where you can still enjoy the traditional Antillean food include the old market hall in Willemstad (Plasa Bieu), Jaanchies Restaurant, Trio Penotti, Restaurant Rozendaels and Seaside Terrace.

International cuisine

Because Curaçao attracts many international visitors, it's not surprising that a lot of restaurants serve mainly international dishes. Most have a varied menu, with a choice of fish, meat and vegetarian dishes. Incidentally, there are also several specialty restaurants that revolve more around Japanese (sushi) or Indonesian dishes, for example.

Our selection of restaurants

We've made an independent selection of 21 restaurants from the many restaurants on Curaçao. This selection is based on several factors. The price/quality ratio and the distinctive character of a restaurant are most important.

The assessments are based on the average of hundreds of reviews. The average price level is determined on the basis of the average price of a main course and can be read as follows:

$ *Main course on average cheaper than USD 16 (approximately NAF 30)*

$$ *Main course average USD 16 to USD 25 (approximately NAF 30 to NAF 45)*

$$$ *Main course on average more expensive than USD 25 (approximately NAF 45)*

Our selection of restaurants

On pages 106/107 you'll find a map with all 21 restaurants that are discussed on the following pages. For the sake of convenience, we've listed them below, in order of geographical location, from west to east.

A. Jaanchies
B. Trio Penotti
C. Landhuis Daniël
D. Karakter
E. Gouverneur de Rouville
F. Plein Café Wilhelmina
G. Munthu Bizarro
H. BijBlauw
I. Scuba Lodge Restaurant
J. Kome
K. Mosa

L. Restaurant Rozendaels
M. Baoase Beach Restaurant
N. Seaside Terrace
O. Origami Sushi
P. Madero Ocean Club
Q. Chill Beach Bar and Grill
R. Landhuis Brakkeput Mei Mei
S. Tabooshh!
T. Zanzibar
U. Omundo

Ⓐ Jaanchies

$ $ $ Avg. rating: ◉◉◉◉○

Jaanchies is a known concept in Curaçao, partly because of the impressive owner (the 'speaking menu'), the whistling sugar snatchers and the decor from grandmother's time. Go here if you've always wanted to eat iguana, or just to have a drink.

◎ WEG NAAR WESTPUNT Z/N   ☏ +599 9 864 0126   🕮 DAILY 12PM - 7PM

Ⓑ Trio Penotti

$ $ $ Avg. rating: ◉◉◉◉◉

This restaurant is a must if you've been to the beaches around Westpunt or Christoffel park for a day. Enjoy a local or international dish on the terrace. Best price/quality ratio on the island!

◎ SAVONET 79, CHRISTOFFEL PARK   ☏ +599 9 513 7535   🕮 TUE - SUN 10AM - 2PM & 5PM - 9PM

Ⓒ Landhuis Daniël

$ $ $ Avg. rating: ◉◉◉◉○

Whether you come by for a cup of coffee with a tasty snack or go for lunch or dinner, at this 18th century mansion you're in the right place. You'll pass Westpunt along the way. The 3-course menu for less than 50 guilders comes highly recommended.

◎ WEG NAAR WESTPUNT Z/N   ☏ +599 9 864 8400   🕮 MON 12PM - 2PM & 5PM - 10PM / TUE - SAT 9AM - 2PM & 5PM - 10PM / SUN 9AM - 10PM

Karakter

$ $ $ Avg. rating:

Away from the crowds, right at sea, is the terrace that belongs to Karakter. If you eat here, you can use the beach chairs for free during the day. You need your ID when you enter the resort.

CORAL ESTATE RESORT, ST. WILLIBRORDUS   +599 9 864 2233   DAILY 8AM - 10PM

Gouverneur de Rouville

$ $ $ Avg. rating:

Admire the ships entering Willemstad from a table on the balcony or find a spot in the beautiful backyard. End your evening in the cocktail bar next door. It's a good idea to reserve ahead if you want to dine on the balcony.

DE ROUVILLEWEG 9-F, OTROBANDA   +599 9 462 5999   DAILY 10AM - 12AM

⒡ Plein Café Wilhelmina $ $ $ Avg. rating: ◉◉◉◉○

Fancy a simple but tasty bite or a refreshing drink? You can! In the heart of Punda all day on the cozy terrace of this typical dutch eatery. They also offer a cheap daily menu (first come first served!).

⊙ WILHELMINAPLEIN 19-23, PUNDA   ☏ +599 9 461 9666   🕐 DAILY 7AM - 10PM

⒢ Mundo Bizarro $ $ $ Avg. rating: ◉◉◉○○

If you didn't know better you'd swear that you've arrived in Cuba. The colorful and cozy interior makes Mundo Bizarro a unique restaurant experience, especially if you're here during one of the weekly live music sessions on Saturday.

⊙ NIEUWESTRAAT 12, PUNDA   ☏ +599 9 461 6767   🕐 DAILY 8AM - 10PM

BijBlauw

$ $ $ Avg. rating: ◉◉◉◉◉

In a courtyard between the monumental buildings of the Pietermaai district in Willemstad you can enjoy a farm-fresh breakfast or a high-quality lunch or dinner directly by the sea. If you want to dine right by the sea, reserve a table in advance.

◎ PIETERMAAI 82-84   ✆ +599 9 650 0551   🕐 DAILY 7AM - 2:30PM & 6PM - 10PM

Scuba Lodge Restaurant

$ $ $ Avg. rating: ◉◉◉◉○

Enjoy the sunset, with your feet in the sand, the sound of the sea in combination with a snack and a drink. Experience the true Caribbean atmosphere and hospitality. Try the famous breakfast basket or the extensive bbq evening.

◎ PIETERMAAI 104   ✆ +599 9 465 2575   🕐 DAILY 7:30AM - 12AM

Ⓙ Kome

$ $ $ Avg. rating: ◉◉◉◉◉

In the Pietermaai district you can find the Kome restaurant. The strength of this restaurant is the creative chef who has put together an original menu. The popular tapas evening takes place on Wednesdays. Reservations recommended.

⊙ JOHAN VAN WALBEECKPLEIN 6, PIETERMAAI   ☏ +599 9 465 0413   🕑 MON - FRI 12PM - 2:30PM / TUE - SAT 6PM - 10PM / SAT FROM 11AM

Ⓚ Mosa

$ $ $ Avg. rating: ◉◉◉◉◉

At the Mosa creativity and quality go hand in hand. The monthly rotating menu consists of smaller dishes that you share with each other. Tapas, not the famous Spanish dishes but other culinary delights.

⊙ PENSTRAAT 41   ☏ +599 9 668 0232   🕑 TUE - SUN 6:30PM - 10:30PM

Restaurant Rozendaels

$ $ $ Avg. rating: ●●●●○

Romantic dining in a Curaçaon ambiance is possible in the beautiful little garden at this restaurant. Choose one of the intimate seating areas and enjoy both local and international dishes. Rozendaels is located just outside the center of Willemstad.

PENSTRAAT 47   +599 9 461 8806   SUN - FRI 5PM - 10PM

Baoase Beach Restaurant

$ $ $ Avg. rating: ●●●●●

According to many, Baoase is the best restaurant in Curaçao (also reflected in the price tag). The decor is beautiful and includes asian influences. Every Sunday the regular menu is replaced by an Asian menu, which includes sushi.

WINTERSWIJKSTRAAT 2   +599 9 461 1799   DAILY 7AM - 10PM

Ⓝ Seaside Terrace

$ $ $ Avg. rating: ◉◉◉◉◯

A sea container that has been converted into a kitchen, a few plastic chairs and some lights. And delicious fresh fish in combination with an extremely relaxed atmosphere. Experience the Antillean hospitality on a small bay just outside Willemstad.

⊙ DR MARTIN LUTHER KING BLVD   📞 +599 9 461 8361   🕐 TUE - SUN 12PM - 10PM

Ⓞ Origami Sushi

$ $ $ Avg. rating: ◉◉◉◉◯

Curaçao only has a few sushi restaurants. The quality on offer at Origami is excellent but, especially in the weekends, you have to take your time. The terrace is shared with another restaurant, so not everyone has to order sushi.

⊙ MAMBO BEACH BOULEVARD   📞 +599 9 461 9009   🕐 DAILY 11AM - 12AM

Madero Ocean Club

$ $ $ Avg. rating:

You can go to Mambo Beach in this trendy open-air restaurant any time in the day. Dinner is of high quality with a wide choice of fish, meat and vegetarian dishes. There's also live music on Wednesdays, Fridays and Sundays.

MAMBO BEACH BOULEVARD   +599 9 465 0073   DAILY 10AM - 12AM / SAT & SUN UNTIL 2AM

Chill Beach Bar and Grill

$ $ $ Avg. rating:

After a day of sunbathing on Mambo Beach, there's nothing better than falling into one of the chill hammocks with an ice cold beer or a nice cocktail. Hungry? Enjoy the famous fish and meat skewers at one of the picnic tables.

MAMBO BEACH BOULEVARD   +599 9 434 8888   DAILY 9AM - 10PM / WED UNTIL 7PM

ⓡ Landhuis Brakkeput Mei Mei $ $ $ Avg. rating: ⬤⬤⬤◯◯

On the terrace of this historic mansion you can eat dishes prepared on a traditional charcoal grill. In addition Mei Mei also has an open-air theater, an 18-hole mini-golf course and a tropical playground.

⊙ KAMINDA BRUDERNAN DI BRAKKAPOTI   ☎ +599 9 767 1500   ⊙ DAILY 6PM - 11PM

ⓢ Tabooshh! $ $ $ Avg. rating: ⬤⬤⬤⬤◯

The atmospheric floating terrace at this restaurant, right on the Spanish Water, serves surprising and original dishes and tapas. If you're staying in or around Jan Thiel district, you can arrange, by phone, to be picked up and brought back home.

⊙ CARACASBAAIWEG 407N   ☎ +599 9 747 5555   ⊙ DAILY 5PM - 10:30PM / SAT & SUN 12PM - 10:30PM

Zanzibar

$ $ $ Avg. rating: ◉◉◉◉○

Zanzibar is an informal, cozy family restaurant. They serve baked pizzas in the stone oven (takeaway available) but there are also meat and fish dishes included on the menu. There is live music on Wednesday evenings. Get a high table on the beach!

◎ JAN THIEL BEACH   ☎ +599 9 747 0633   🕐 DAILY 8AM - 12AM

Omundo

$ $ $ Avg. rating: ◉◉◉◉◉

Stylish yet cozy, with no less than 20 wines that can be ordered by the glass. On Tuesdays and Thursdays you can enjoy swinging live music from 10PM. Every Friday they also have live music outside on the terrace from 5PM.

◎ SUIKERTUINTJEWEG   ☎ +599 9 738 8477   🕐 MON - SAT 10AM - 12AM / TUE & THU UNTIL 2AM

Photo: Berber van Beek

Nightlife and events

When the sun sets at 7 o'clock in the evening, the Curaçaoans sound in the nightlife. This has been happening for years during the famous happy hours. Every day of the week there is a beach bar that keeps happy hour by night. The drinks are then half the price, for an hour, the music goes a tad louder and the feet start to move on the dancefloor. Even after the happy hours the night has plenty to offer: go salsa dancing at a salsa workshop, drink cocktails in Pietermaai or dance the night away in one of Curaçao's nightclubs.

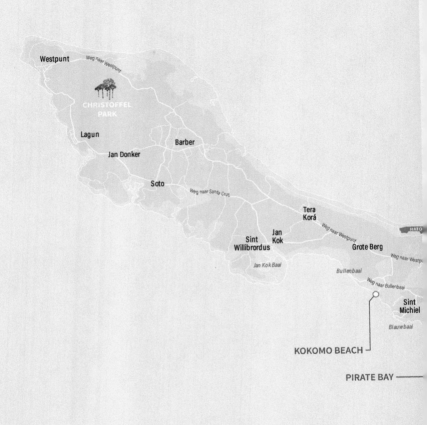

Westpunt

Weg naar Westpunt

CHRISTOFFEL PARK

Lagun

Jan Donker

Barber

Soto

Weg naar Santa Cruz

Tera Korá

Weg naar Westpunt

HATO

Sint Willibrordus

Jan Kok

Grote Berg

Weg naar Westpunt

Jan Kok Baai

Bullenbaai

Weg naar Bullenbaai

Sint Michiel

Blauwbaai

KOKOMO BEACH

PIRATE BAY

Overview of nightlife locations on Curaçao

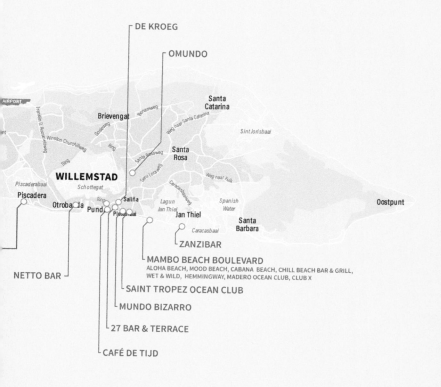

Happy hours

Happy hours are popular on Curaçao. This isn't only due to the favorable prices, but also because happy hours guarantee a pleasant crowd. The volume goes to level ten or a band or DJ will play live. At some beach spots there are snacks around or the barbecue is getting started. Below you'll find an overview of the best happy hours. For a complete overview, check out the free magazine available everywhere on the island: PasaBon, or online pasabon.com.

Kokomo Beach

On Sunday evening from 5pm to 6pm, happy hour takes place at Kokomo Beach with live music. Kokomo Beach is located west of Willemstad, halfway to the Weg naar Bullenbaai. Kokomo opened its doors in 2011. It is a concept on the island, not only as a beach, but also as a place of entertainment. In addition, you can dine between 6pm and 9.30pm from Tuesday to Saturday. Every month you also have the famous full moon party. View the website for the events calendar.

⚓ **Kokomo Beach**
Happy hour: Sun 5PM - 6PM | Address: Vaersenbaai | Website: www.kokomo-beach.com

Mambo Beach Boulevard

On the beach at Mambo Beach Boulevard there are several beach clubs that keep happy hours at different times. On Saturday you can go to *Aloha Beach* and *Madero Ocean Club* from 5pm to 6pm.

Especially on Sundays this beach is the place to be. Step out to *Cabana Beach* or *Madero Ocean Club* at 2pm. There is a mojito bar and they offer tasty snacks fresh from the grill. At 6pm, perhaps the best-known and most fun happy hour on the island gets underway: *Wet & Wild*. The happy hour here really is a party you don't want to miss. They play nice music and there's a spacious dance floor complete with disco lights. Not only on Sundays, but the whole weekend here is an experience. You can carry on till late in the night, but you can also go to one of the many restaurants for a dinner with live music in the background.

At *Hemmingway restaurant and bar* you can listen to live reggae, piano and salsa music from 7pm on Friday to Sunday respectively. Of course, feel free to dance around.

So for a nice drink or a fun night out until the early hours, you can indulge yourself at the beach of Mambo Beach Boulevard.

Mambo Beach Boulevard

Happy hours: see above | Address: Bapor Kibra | Website: www.blvdcuracao.com

Pirate Bay

Every Friday, this beach club, located in the Piscadera bay to the west of Willemstad, has an extra-long happy hour from 5pm to 7pm. There's live music and at Pirate Bay you dance in the sand. Pirate Bay is also a restaurant with an extensive menu. The staff is remarkably friendly. As the name suggests, it's like you've arrived on the set of the Pirates of the Caribbean. The grinning pirate dolls complete the picture with the dark interior and the metal chandeliers. Pirate Bay also organizes other events in addition to the happy hours.

Pirate Bay

Happy hour: Fri 5PM - 7PM | Address: Piscadera Bay | Website: piratebaycuracao.com

Zanzibar

Every Saturday from 5pm to 6pm it's happy hour at Zanzibar. This happy hour is also one of the busiest on the island. There are often live bands or DJs and there are snacks from the barbecue. In addition to regular happy hours, they also regularly host events, parties and concerts. Zanzibar is located in the Jan Thielbaai. You can have dinner at Zanzibar, or one of the other restaurants nearby, so for convenience, you can pull up a chair after you've had a drink or two.

Zanzibar
Happy hour: Sat 5PM - 6PM | Address: Jan Thielbaai | Website: www.beach-restaurants.com

Café De Tijd

In Pietermaai you'll find the typical Dutch pub Café De Tijd. On Thursday evening the extra-long happy hour is from 9pm to 11pm and there will be a DJ the whole evening. Café De Tijd is open daily from 4pm to 3am and in the weekend it's open till 4pm. It's a popular café among students and tourists.

Café De Tijd
Happy hour: Thu 9PM - 11PM | Address: Pietermaai | Website: www.facebook.com/cafedetijd

Saint Tropez Ocean Club

Every Friday evening they have no less than two happy hours: from 6pm to 7pm and from 9pm to 10pm. There's a DJ from 10pm until 1am. During the first happy hour they serve small snacks. From 8pm you can smoke a water pipe in the lounge area. Events are also organized on other days.

Saint Tropez also has an extensive, international menu and you can go there from breakfast to dinner. The club is located on the water in Pietermaai and has a beautiful view of the sea. There's an infinity pool in the middle of the club where, in the daytime, it resembles the French Riviera. Around the pool you have loungers and cabanas to dream away while the sun goes down on the edge of Willemstad.

Saint Tropez Ocean Club
Happy hours: Fri 6PM - 7PM & 9PM - 10PM | Address: Pietermaai 152 | Website: Sainttropezcuracao.com

Mundo Bizarro

Every day between 5.30pm and 6.30pm, this Cuban café/restaurant has happy hour, with live music on Saturdays. Mundo Bizarro is located in Pietermaai, and besides tasty drinks, it also has a great kitchen. So afterwards, a delicious dinner is a good option. See also page 112.

Mundo Bizarro
Address: Nieuwstraat 12 (Pietermaai) | Website www.mundobizarrocuracao.com

Going out

After a drink during one of the happy hours, you can continue until the early hours in the weekends. We've made a selection of the nicest bars and nightclubs for you to visit.

Netto Bar

Netto Bar, the brownest pub on the island, is part of the fabric of Curaçao. The bar was founded by the late Ernesto 'Netto' Koster, an icon in Willemstad. Net's biggest dream was to run a bar in his own neighborhood. In 1954 he made his dream come true and he worked in the Netto Bar until he was 87 years old. The bar is worth a visit for the interior alone. The bar is full of pictures and paintings of the idyllic Curaçao and of Netto with famous guests in his bar, like the Dutch King Willem Alexander. On Friday night there is often live music and the feet get moving on the dancefloor. While enjoying the bright green, homemade drinks known as Róm Bèrdè, you can dance the night away.

Netto Bar
Address: Breedestraat 143 (Otrobanda) | Website: www.nettobar.com

27 Bar & Terrace

In the heart of Punda is 27 Bar & Terrace, named after the legendary club of 27. Artists who have the dubious honor of belonging to this club all died when they were 27, including Jimi Hendrix, Janis Joplin, Jim Morrison, Kurt Cobain and more recently Amy Winehouse. 27 is the only rock & roll club on the island, where many a live band treat the visitors to original performances of famous songs. They also have regular jam sessions with local artists. Every day there's a happy hour between 6pm and 7pm. There's also live music from Thursday to Saturday.

ⓘ **27 Bar & Terrace**
   Address: De Ruyterkade (Pietermaai) | Website: www.27curacao.com

Omundo

Every Tuesday and Thursday is dedicated to live music. These evenings, also known as *Omundo Grooves*, offer piano, live performances by local singers and artists, and there is a DJ. The musical styles mainly stem from South America, such as, for example, Latin, Salsa and Soul music. Because Omundo is also a restaurant, you can combine an evening out with a dinner. See also page 119.

ⓘ **Omundo**
   Address: Zuikertuintje | Website: www.omundocuracao.com

De Kroeg ('The Pub')

Although the name doesn't suggest it, De Kroeg is a very special location. De Kroeg is on a ship that is anchored in the Waaigat in Willemstad. On Thursdays to Saturdays, you can party until four in the morning to a variety of musical styles, from techno to salsa. They also organize other events, including a good old-fashioned bingo night on the first Wednesday of every month. Check De Kroeg's Facebook page for current information and announcements.

De Kroeg
Address: Waaigatplein (ship next to parking lot 'Plaza Mundo Merced')
Website: www.facebook.com/dekroegcuracao

Annual events

Perhaps the most famous and fun annual event is carnival. We already described this on page 26. But besides carnival there are also a number of other fun events you don't want to miss out on, provided you are in Curaçao at the time of course.

New year's eve

There are a lot of fireworks on show on the island in the days leading up to New Year's Eve. In particular, the pagaras, deafening 100,000 firecrackers, can be heard and felt everywhere. Various large fireworks shows are organized in and around Willemstad.

From time to time there are beach concerts by popular, mostly Dutch, artists and DJs. Keep an eye on the announcements on the island to see where you need to be and make sure to buy your concert tickets in time.

Fuikdag

On the first Sunday of the new year, when the champagne and new year's eve snacks are still being digested, Curaçaon partygoers head to Fuikbaai. This bay transforms into an unorganized chaos of boats and party people. In recent years there have been several top DJs such as Afrojack and Martin Garrix who put on a surprise live performance, from their own boat or from the floating stage. You can only come here by boat. So you can rent a boat yourself, but there are also boat owners who sell spots on their private boats.

Kings' Day

The population of Curaçao is very much a fan of royalty, evident from the many state portraits you encounter in government buildings, among other things. As such, King's Day doesn't pass by quietly on Curaçao. All of Willemstad turns orange on King's Day, with lots of market stalls and bands filling the streets. Top Dutch artists regularly give concerts on King's Day or the night before. Especially in Pietermaai, King's night is celebrated exuberantly.

Curaçao North Sea Jazz Festival

Every year (since 2010) at the end of August / beginning of September, Curaçao organizes a special edition of the North Sea Jazz festival with world-class artists. In the past this has included names such as Tom Jones, Lenny Kravitz, Lionel Richie, John Legend, Sting and Jason Derulo.

ⓘ **Curaçao North Sea Jazz Festival**
  Location: World Trade Center Curaçao | Website & tickets: www.curacaonorthseajazz.com

Cinemas

Cinemas

Curaçao has three large cinemas, of which two are located in Willemstad. We'll describe the main characteristics of these cinemas.

THE MOVIES

The Movies is the oldest cinema in Curaçao, but it's still modern. Although the building looks traditional, the rooms are equipped with the latest visual and audio technology. They also show 3D-movies here. The scheduling of both cinemas is well coordinated with minimal overlap, so the full range of movies on offer on Curaçao is quite extensive.

The Movies
Address: Plaza Mundo Merced (Scharloo) | Website incl. movie calendar: www.themoviescuracao.com

THE CINEMAS

The Cinemas opened its doors in 2009 and is part of the big Renaissance hotel in Otrobanda. The cinema is equipped with no fewer than six different halls, all fitted with digital screens and perfect sound. 3D-movies are shown in two of the halls.

The Cinemas
Address: Baden Powellweg 1 (Renaissance Riffort) | Website incl. movie calendar: Thecinemascuracao.com

CINEMARK

Cinemark is the newest cinema in Curaçao and is located in Sambil, the huge shopping mall, just a ten-minute drive west of Willemstad. This is the cinema of all cinemas, with comfortable leather seats, perfect picture and sound quality and, last but not least, so-called D-box chairs. These chairs move in sync with the movie, for an even more intense experience.

Cinemark
Address: Veeris 27 (Sambil) | Website incl. movie calendar: www.cinemarkca.com

Don't forget to put on long pants or other warm clothes before you go to the movies, the cinema halls can be quite chilly with the air conditioning.

Route I

The 'wild west' of Curaçao

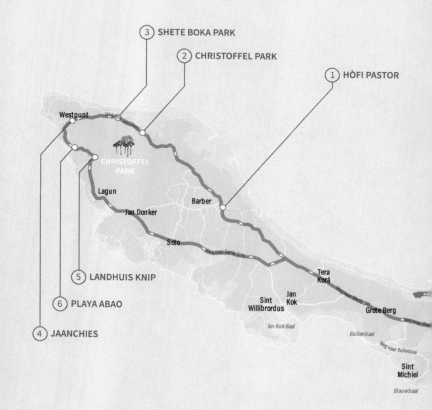

① HÒFI PASTOR

② CHRISTOFFEL PARK

③ SHETE BOKA PARK

④ JAANCHIES

⑤ LANDHUIS KNIP

⑥ PLAYA ABAO

Westpunt

CHRISTOFFEL PARK

Lagun

Jan Donker

Barber

Soto

Tera Korá

Sint Willibrordus

Jan Kok

Jan Kok Baai

Grote Berg

Bullenbaai

Weg naar Bullenbaai

Sint Michiel

Blauwbaai

The 'wild west' of Curaçao

As soon as you drive 15 minutes west of Willemstad, there isn't much left of the picturesque city center, the tourist attractions or the beautiful little restaurants. The west side of the island - apart from the occasional small sleepy village - is unspoilt and remote. Nature is in charge here and determines the surroundings. Of course there is plenty of fun to be had along the coast on the dozens of beaches but, if you follow this route, you'll discover that the outback also has its charm and a lot of beauty to offer.

Although the distances on Curaçao are relatively small, a single journey to Westpoint takes just under an hour. The roads are not all of equal quality yet and motorways don't exist in Curaçao. On average, people drive 50 mph (80 km/h) on the main roads.

About this route
We start the route in Willemstad. At the top of each page you can find the directions, with an indication of the duration of the route. This route takes a full day, but can be cut short, if desired, by skipping certain parts.

It's a good idea to get a detailed road map of Curaçao in addition to the directions in this book.

Willemstad → Hòfi Pastor

From Otrobanda, exit the roundabout at the bus station on *Pater Eeuwensweg*.

This road runs parallel with the coast, and leads you along the neighborhoods of *Piscadera* and *Julianadorp* until the roundabout, from which you need to follow the *Weg naar Westpunt*.

After about 30 minutes you will reach the village of *Barber* where you'll find the entrance to *Hòfi Pastor* next to the church.

30 min

- ## Hòfi Pastor

  Hòfi Pastor is a hiking/walking area with a fairytale atmosphere. The area owes its fame mainly to the ancient and gigantic *Kapok tree*. This is the oldest tree on the island and very impressive to see. A hiking route has been set out through the fairytale forests that takes about half an hour. During this walk you also have the possibility to enjoy a picnic, or something to drink (bring your own).

Hòfi Pastor → Christoffel Park

From Hòfi Pastor you continue the *Weg naar Westpunt*. After about ten minutes you'll see signs for *Christoffel Park*.

On the right side of the *Weg naar Westpunt* is a parking lot and an office. Here you can pay for the entrance to the Christoffel Park and buy a map.

10
min

• Christoffel Park

The park has one main road that runs in a large loop and ends at the entrance. Along the main road there are several parking places to stop and take a walk through the park.

You can of course go hiking through the park, but you can also book a jeep safari. On the way you'll get to hear a lot about all the flora and fauna in the park. For the more active traveler, there's also the possibility to climb the Christoffel Mountain. For more information about Christoffel Park, see page 70.

- ## Shete Boka Park

Although you can choose to leave your car in the main parking lot and take a walk along the bokas (inlets), this is not recommended: the distances between the bokas are quite big and limestone plains get hot in the middle of the day.

The best way to see the different bokas is by car: you can park your car at every boka, and then explore it on foot.

Tip: preferably visit the Shete Boka Park on a day with lots of wind, this makes it even more spectacular! See also page 72.

Hungry or thirsty? Restaurant Joanchies is on this route, see page 110.

Shete Boka Park → Landhuis Knip

From the *Shete Boka Park* follow the *Weg naar Westpunt* towards Westpunt. After a few minutes you'll see restaurant *Joanchies* on the left.

15 min

You will then pass by, among other things, *Westpunt* and *Playa Forti*. Here it's possible to, at your own risk, take a jump in the sea from a height of 40 feet. At Playa Forti (see also page 47) there's another good local restaurant where you can go for lunch or a drink. After a few miles follow the signs to *Landhuis ('mansion') Knip*.

- Landhuis Knip

Landhuis Knip is a historic building near the most western point of Curaçao. The mansion owes its fame to the slave revolt that started in 1795 from the plantations at Knip.

Tula is the person who led the slave revolt and he is still remembered by many as a hero. The mansion houses a museum, which revolves around Tula. See also page 85.

Landhuis Knip → Playa Abao (Grote Knip)

From Landhuis Knip follow the signs to *Playa Abao*.

Playa Abao is at the end of the road that leads through the plantations at Knip. At the beginning of this road you can also turn left at the T-junction, you will arrive at a very small beach, called *Kleine Knip*.

Finally, continue on the main road to head back to Willemstad. Via the *Weg naar Sta. Cruz* you'll end up on the *Weg naar Westpunt*. Follow the signs for Willemstad.

• Playa Abao (Grote Knip)

Playa Abao is part of the plantations that belong to Knip. The beach is therefore also called 'Knip', or 'Kenepa', named after fruit produced by the Kenepa tree that grows in this area. After the strenuous activities of the day, it's wonderful to have a tasty snack at Playa Abao and of course take a refreshing dip. See also page 47.

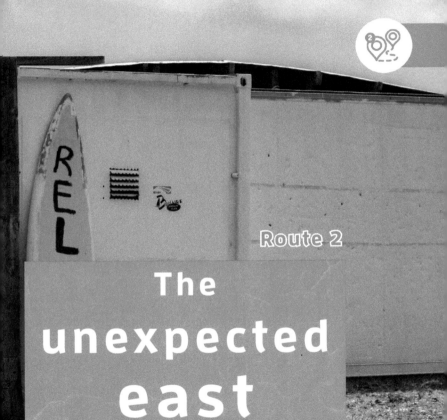

Route 2

The
unexpected
east
of Curaçao

Westpunt

Weg naar Westpunt

CHRISTOFFEL
PARK

Lagun

Jan Donker

Barber

Soto

Weg naar Santa Cruz

Tera
Korá

Sint
Willibrordus

Jan
Kok

Weg naar Westpunt

Grote Berg

Weg naar Wes

Jan Kok Baai

Bullenbaai

Weg naar Bullenbaai

Sint
Michiel

Blauwbaai

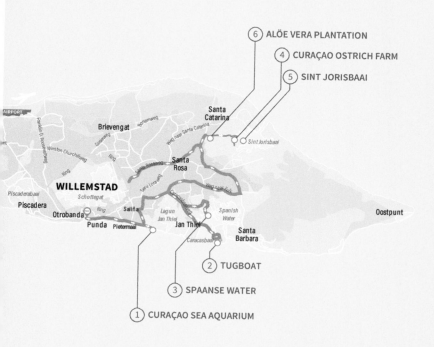

AIRPORT

Piscaderabaai

Piscadera

WILLEMSTAD

Otrobanda

Punda

Pietermaal

Saliña

Schottegat

Brievengat

Santa
Rosa

Santa
Catarina

Lagun
Jan Thiel

Jan Thiel

Spanish
Water

Santa
Barbara

Caracasbaai

Sint Jorisbaai

Oostpunt

Franklin D. Rooseveltweg

Winston Churchillweg

Gosieweg

Ring

Ring

Ring

Ring

Seru Lora weg

Isghamweg

Weg naar Santa Catarina

Weg naar Fuik

⑥ ALÖE VERA PLANTATION

④ CURAÇAO OSTRICH FARM

⑤ SINT JORISBAAI

② TUGBOAT

③ SPAANSE WATER

① CURAÇAO SEA AQUARIUM

The unexpected east of Curaçao

The east side of Curaçao is a place with many contrasts. Whereas the immediate surroundings of Willemstad are fully developed, just a few miles away, you'll encounter fewer and fewer houses. More towards the north-east the area even looks a bit like Texas: dry, desolate and an occasional stray dog. The most expensive resorts and villa parks are also located on the east side of the island.

This route shows you the surprising contrasts on the east side of the island, fun for both young and old. Don't forget to bring your snorkel set.

About this route

We start the route in Willemstad. At the top of each page you can find the directions, with an indication of the duration of the route. This route takes a full day, but can be cut short, if desired, by skipping certain parts.

It's a good idea to get a detailed road map of Curaçao in addition to the directions in this book.

Willemstad → Curaçao Sea Aquarium

From Punda drive out of Willemstad via the *Pietermaai* street and *Penstraat*. Continue on this road along the coast.

At the end of this road you'll arrive at the car park for the *Sea Aquarium Park Curaçao*, where you can park your car for NAF 5.

- ## Curaçao Sea Aquarium

The Curaçao Sea Aquarium is a tourist attraction and an absolute must for any vacationer on the island. The various aquariums are home to a variety of (underwater) animals from around Curaçao. Get to know the underwater world of the Caribbean in a fun way.

It's much more fun to attend a number of training demonstrations with sea lions or dolphins. You can also help with feeding the flamingos, for example. Many people dream of swimming with dolphins. Reservations required. See also page 74.

Curaçao Sea Aquarium → Tugboat

Drive back on the same road you took and after appr. 1/4 mile turn right in *Koraalspechtweg*.

Turn right at the end and then take an immediate left in the *Dominguitoweg*. At the end, turn right into the *Caracasbaaiweg*. At the roundabout all the way at the end of this road, turn left.

Approximately 150 feet before the end of this road, turn left and at the end turn right again. Drive left around the big house (bad road), and park at the *Tugboat Beach Bar*.

20
min

• Tugboat

The tugboat is a well-known snorkeling spot on Curaçao. You can go snorkeling or diving to a sunken tugboat. The boat is just below the water surface and is covered with coral. There are always many fish to be found here and it's a hot spot for snorkeling.

Be careful not to touch the boat, the coral that is on it can cause irritation, and the material is very fragile.

Hungry or thirsty? Eat or drink something at the Tugboat Beach Bar.

Tugboat → Spanish Water

Drive back via the same road, and at the roundabout turn right back to the *Caracasbaaiweg*. After about 1/2 mile, turn right onto the *Kaminda Brudernan di Brakepoti*. Take the fourth exit on the right, go right again at the end. A road map can be useful for this part of the route.

Follow this road until you see *Sail Adventure Curaçao* on the right. This is located directly on the Spanish Water. Here you can rent a boat.

- **Spanish Water**

The Spanish Water is a vast inland water area, which opens out to the sea. The best thing is to explore the Spanish Water with a boat: at *Sail Adventure Curaçao* you can rent several motor and sailing boats, to explore the Spanish Water on your own (or with skipper if you prefer), see page 66.

Take some sandwiches and drinks with you, and enjoy a unique lunch during your trip. Along the water there are many spacious villas, one even larger and more impressive than the next.

Hungry or thirsty? *Restaurant Zambezi at the Ostrich Farm is recommended!*

Spanish Water → Ostrich Farm

Drive back to the *Caracasbaaiweg*, and turn right towards Willemstad. After a few hundred yards turn right onto *Sta. Barbara* (follow the signs).

Past the entrance of the *Santa Barbara resort* turn left into the *Weg naar Sta. Barbara*. After a few miles follow the signs for *Ostrich Farm*.

🚗 25 min

• Ostrich Farm

Ostriches on a tropical island like Curaçao? The Ostrich Farm shows that this is a great concept. Every hour a safari truck leaves for a tour along the ostrich fields. During the tour you can get to know these peculiar animals in a fun way.

During a visit to the Ostrich Farm, you'll be forgiven for feeling like you've briefly left Curaçao. The surroundings sooner resemble the nature of Africa. See also page 76.

An alternative to the Ostrich Farm is the nearby Aloe Vera Plantation, here you can learn everything about this plant and its medicinal effects.

3
min

Ostrich Farm → Sint Jorisbaai

Continue the road along the Ostrich Farm and you will arrive at *Sint Jorisbaai*.

To drive back from Sint Joris Bay to Willemstad, head back and turn left at the main road. At the end of this road you turn right at the *Weg naar Montana* and follow signs for Willemstad.

Sint Jorisbaai

A few hundred yards past the Ostrich Farm is St. George's Bay. It's a good kitesurfing spot. A spectacular sport to watch, or to try out yourself.

If you want to give it a try it is wise to arrange a lesson. See also page 64.

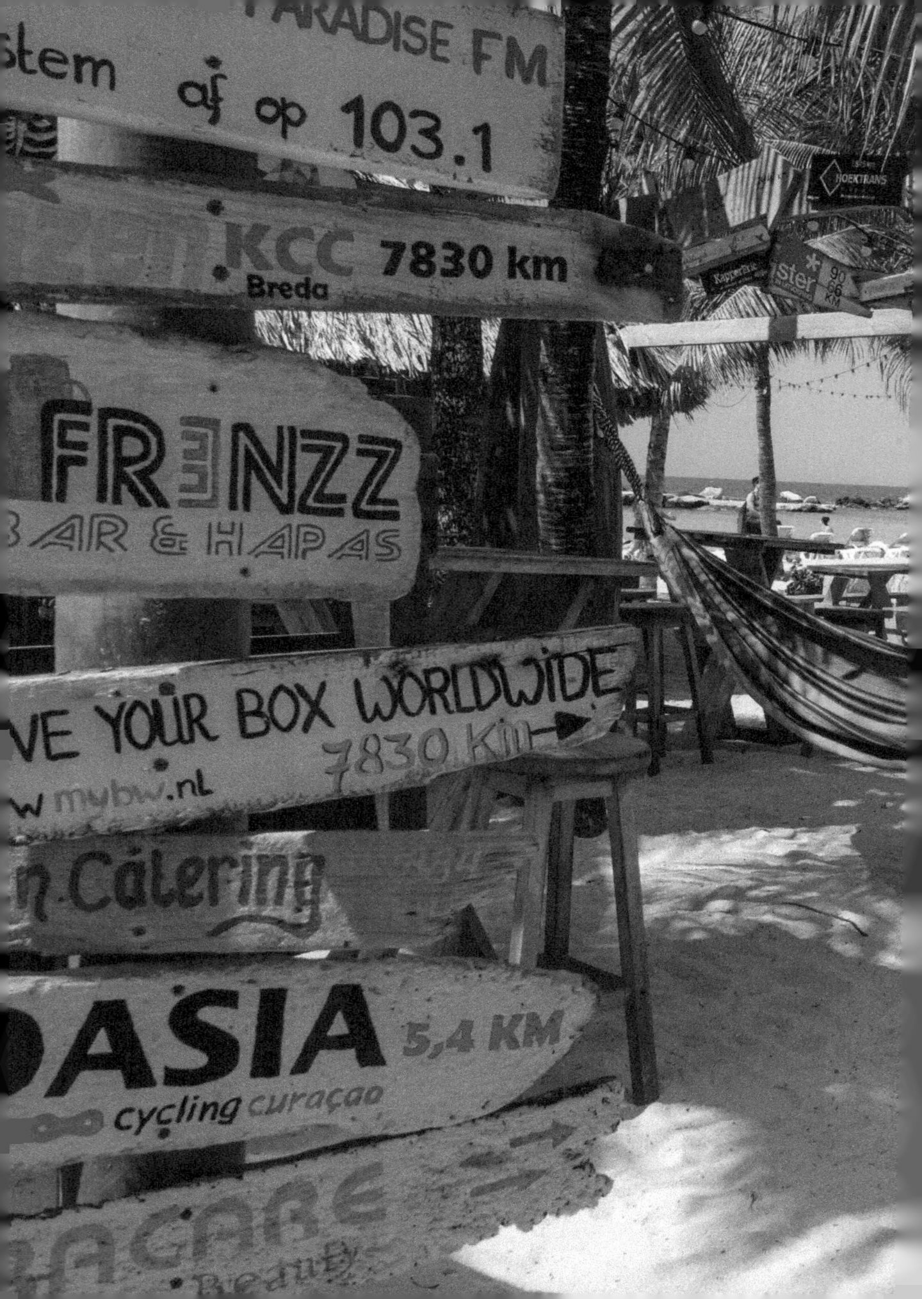

PARADISE FM
stem af op 103.1

KCC 7830 km
Breda

FRENZZ
BAR & HAPAS

VE YOUR BOX WORLDWIDE
7830 KM
w mybw.nl

n Catering

OASIA 5,4 KM
cycling curaçao

Practical information

Can I connect my telephone charger to a power
socket in Curaçao? What should I do if I have a car
accident? What currency do they use on Curaçao?
Can I just pay with my credit card? Where can I find
the best supermarkets and when are they open?

You'll find an answer to this and other practical
questions in this chapter.

Language: learn some Papiamento!

Although the locals mostly speak Papiamento, almost everyone speaks Dutch and/or English, but it is highly appreciated if you, as a visitor, can speak a few words of Papiamento.

The signage on Curaçao is always in Dutch. Many signs have been placed along the roads in recent years to indicate the routes to beaches, restaurants and other places of interest. Menus are always in Dutch or English.

List of words

English	Papiaments	English	Papiaments
Welcome	Bon bini	Pharmacy	Botica
Good morning.	Bon dia	House	Kas
Good afternoon,	Bon tardi	Map	Mapa
Good evening	Bon nochi	Suitcase	Falis
Bye!	Ayo!	Police	Polis
		Check	Kuenta
How's everything going?	Kon ta bai?	Beach	Playa
		Hill/mountain	Seru
All is well!	Mi ta bon		
Thank you	Danki	One	Un
You're welcome	Di nada	Two	Dos
		Three	Tres
Yes	Si	Four	Kuater
No	Nò	Five	Sinku
Good	Bon	Six	Seis
Many	Hopi	Seven	Siete
Little	Tiki	Eight	Ocho
Please	Por fabor	Nine	Nuebe
Where is... ?	Unda ta…	Ten	Dies
Excuse me	Despensa	Hundred	Cien
Very nice	Hopi dushi		

Transport on Curaçao

Public transport

There are several bus lines on Curaçao and there are also minibuses around. The large bus lines run on fixed routes and don't deviate, but usually only run once an hour or sometimes even less. The minibuses don't run according to fixed times, but due to the large number of minibuses you never have to wait long.

The route the minibuses take is indicated with a sign behind the windshield and they can be recognized by the word *'BUS'* on the license plate. One of the advantages of these minibuses is that the drivers - sometimes for a small fee – can deviate from the route and drop you off somewhere. Payment is made in cash to the driver, a ride of about 20 minutes costs a few Antillean guilders.

There are two bus stations in Willemstad. One is in the Punda district, the other in Otrobanda. You can go to the bus station in Otrobanda to see the departure times of the big bus lines.

From Punda the buses leave in the eastern direction of the island. Most tourist areas such as Mambo Beach Boulevard and Jan Thiel are easily accessible from Willemstad by public transport. Keep in mind that after ten o'clock in the evening there's no more public transport on the island!

The Otrobanda district is to the west side of the island. The minibuses only have short routes here, while the big buses run all the way to Westpunt. The disadvantage is that most of the beaches are a few miles away from the main road (at least half an hour's walk). Therefore public transport is less suitable to discover the west side of Curaçao.

Taxis
There are plenty of taxis available on Curaçao. There are taxi stands at the airport, in Willemstad, at many hotels and at the nightlife hubs. Not all taxis run on a meter, but run according to fixed rates. From the airport to Willemstad (Otrobanda) you pay an average of NAF 55 (about $ 30). You pay about NAF 70 to Mambo Beach Boulevard and about NAF 80 to Jan Thiel. You can recognize official taxis by checking the number plate which starts with *TX*.

Rental cars
Although Curaçao offers some opportunities to find your way around the island with the help of public transport and taxis, you really need your own transport to truly explore the island. There are several well-known car rental companies at the airport, which generally offer a well-maintained fleet of vehicles.

It is advisable to ask for the most important traffic rules when renting a car, these differ slightly from the American and European traffic regulations. In case of wet road surfaces, pay extra attention, because the roads can be very slippery due to oil residue!

Money on Curaçao

The guilder

The local currency on Curaçao is the Dutch-Antillean Florin (NAF), also called the Antillean Dutch Guilder (ANG). The exchange rate of the Antillean guilder is linked to the US dollar at a fixed exchange rate. This price is set at $ 1 is NAF 1.78. In many places it's also possible to pay with US dollars, as they circulate freely.

ATMs

On Curaçao there are plenty of banks and ATMs where you can withdraw money in local currency or in US dollars. For this, depending on the bank, a surcharge can be charged.

It's also possible to pay with your credit card all over the island.

Supermarkets

The supermarkets on Curaçao are influenced by both the Dutch and the American market. You can see these influences in the range and quantity of products and goods, but also in the design and appearance of the store. Most supermarkets are pretty large and they also sell many non-food items.

Most products are imported from America and Europe. Most vegetables and most fruit is supplied by ship from South America.

The following supermarkets are the best choice for holidaymakers due to their location, wide range and quality of products:

Centrum Supermarket, two branches:
1. Weg naar Bullenbaai, near Piscadera and Blue Bay just west of Willemstad
Open: Mon - Fri 7.30am - 7.30pm, Sat 7.30am - 8.00pm, Sun 7.30am - 5.00pm
2. SBN Doormanweg, Mahaai
Open: Mon - Sat 7.30am - 8.00pm, Sun 7.30am - 5.00pm

Van den Tweel, two branches:
1. Kaya Damasco, Jan Thiel
Open: daily 8.00am - 9.00pm
2. Kaya Jacob Posner, Zeelandia, near Willemstad and Mambo BLVD
Open: daily 7.30am – 8.30pm

Apart from *Centrum* and *Van den Tweel*, the supermarkets *Vreugdenhil* and *Best Buy* are also recommended. Most supermarkets can be found in the surroundings of Willemstad, in the direction of Westpunt you'll find just a few small stores.

Drinking water & electricity

On Curaçao, the seawater is purified using a unique and costly process. The result is excellent drinkable tap water, known as the cleanest water in the Caribbean.

Because desalinating the seawater is a very costly process, the tariffs for water consumption are considerably higher than in the USA. Using water economically is therefore a must in Curaçao and par for the course.

Electricity
The grid voltage on Curaçao is 110 volts/50Hz, although many hotels and apartments have a European 220 volt outlet. Many electrical appliances, laptops and cameras can easily be connected to 220 volts, but depending on your accommodation, the sockets are sometimes European, for which you need an adapter. These are available on the island for a few guilders.

Renewable energy

Curaçao still has insufficient options for running the electricity grid on green energy. In the nineties, two wind farms were installed along the north coast to generate energy. These wind turbines, however, were unable to withstand the strong winds and the salt coming from the sea, and they were therefore replaced a few years ago by new turbines. The parks are in the direction of Westpunt at *Tera Kora*, and slightly more to the east at *Playa Kanoa*.

Important telephone numbers

Curaçao is equipped with an excellent mobile telephone network, which - with the exception of remote areas - offers network coverage throughout the entire island. Bringing a mobile phone is therefore always recommended in case of emergencies. Curaçao has the following important telephone numbers:

Police and fire department
911

Ambulance
912

Traffic accident
199 (Curaçao Road Service)

Coast Guard
913

The international access number for Curaçao is 00 5999.

Traffic accident
If you're involved in a traffic accident, it's good to know that you should always call Curaçao Road Service on 199 for assistance and help with any material damages, and not the police.

The Curaçao Road Service is the authority in Curaçao that draws up an official damage report, which must also be handed over to the insurance company. Without a damage report from Curaçao Road Service, the car rental company can recover the damages from you, because it is not covered by the insurance!

Index

Below you'll find an overview of locations mentioned throughout this book, as well as some popular keywords.

Beaches

Other locations & keywords

Dear reader,

However we've tried our best to make this book as complete and accurate as we could, it's always possible for some of the content to get outdated.

If you encountered any errors or inaccurate information, please send us an email at **curacao@goodtimeconcepts.nl**.

Suggestions, tips and comments are welcome as well.

Thank you for your cooperation and we wish you a very nice holiday on the beautiful island of Curaçao!

CPSIA information can be obtained
at www.ICGtesting.com
Printed in the USA
BVHW051235131221
623894BV00021B/828